"Es geht auch anders, doch so geht es auch."

Bertolt Brecht
(*Die Dreigroschenoper*)

To Christopher,

with kind wishes,

Stephen Dec. 1971.

UNIVERSITY OF BRISTOL
Department of Philosophy

9 Woodland Road
Bristol
BS8 1TB

CATEGORIAL FRAMEWORKS

CATEGORIAL FRAMEWORKS

STEPHAN KÖRNER

OXFORD
BASIL BLACKWELL
1970

ISBN 0 631 12950 2   Cloth bound edition

ISBN 0 631 13600 2   Paper bound edition

Library of Congress Catalog Card Number:
76–129594

Printed in Great Britain by
William Clowes and Sons, Limited, London and Beccles
and bound by the Kemp Hall Bindery, Oxford

Table of Contents

Table of Contents

Preface

The manner in which a person classifies the objects of his experience into highest classes or categories, the standards of intelligibility which he applies, and the metaphysical beliefs which he holds are intimately related. To give an obvious example, the employment of the category of causally determined events, the demand that all or some explanations be causal, and the belief that nature is at least partly a deterministic system so involve each other that they are either all present in a person's thinking or else all absent from it. Groups of persons, societies, and whole civilizations exhibit, in so far as they can be said to think, a similar correlation between their categories, standards of intelligibility and metaphysical beliefs. The thesis is sufficiently general and imprecise to meet with the approval of most philosophers, historians, anthropologists, and others concerned with the structure and development of thought. It is also sufficiently important and relevant to their interests to deserve detailed examination.

Such an examination requires on the one hand the systematic collection of empirical material, i.e. theories, ideologies, and reports on everyday intellectual habits in their wider contexts; on the other hand the construction, improvement, and analysis of the conceptual apparatus by means of which the empirical material is organized. The two activities are inseparable, but the emphasis may vary. In a logico-philosophical inquiry, such as is undertaken here, the main weight is put on conceptual analysis and theoretical construction. As to his empirical material the inquirer will depend on his first-hand experience of philosophical thinking, on his grasp of the philosophical and non-philosophical theories of others, on selected reports by anthropologists and sociologists, and on selected writings by historians, in particular historians of ideas.

The plan of the essay has been largely determined by its purpose. Chapter I develops the main instrument of the subsequent analyses, namely the notion of a categorial framework, by adopting, adapting, and relativizing certain logical and ontological distinctions due to Aristotle, Kant, Frege, and others. The main aim of chapter II is to distinguish as clearly as possible between the internal and the external view of a categorial system and to dispel various stubborn illusions

X   PREFACE

which have their root in the failure to make this distinction. Chapter III
exhibits some features of the logical and categorial structure of factual
and practical thinking and of their interconnection; chapter IV some
features of the logical and categorial structure of commonsense and
scientific (especially quantitative) thinking. Chapter V contains an
answer to the problem of the relation between a person's use of a
certain categorial framework, his explanatory standards and his metaphysics. Since categorial stability will, at this stage of the argument, have
turned out to be an illusion, the last chapter, i.e. chapter VI, is devoted
to the problem of categorial change and to the rôle played by philosophical arguments in preventing or advancing it. The Appendix contains
a brief, systematic description of the logical systems to which reference
is made in the text.

The essay develops some ideas suggested in chapter I of *Experience
and Theory* (London, 1966) and explained in greater detail in chapters
XI–XIII of *What is Philosophy?—One Philosopher's Answer* (London,
1969). An early version of chapter VI was delivered as a guest-lecture to
the Israel Academy of Sciences and Humanities and published in vol.
III, No. 10 (1969) of the Academy's *Proceedings*. I am grateful to its
Secretary for his kind permission to use this material.

My thanks are also due to three friends and colleagues at Bristol
University, Dr. John Cleave of the Department of Mathematics, Mr.
Robert Kirkham of the Department of Philosophy, and Professor John
Ziman of the Department of Physics, who have made helpful comments
on an early draft. In this connection it is particularly gratifying to be
able to refer readers with a specialist interest in logic to a paper by
Dr. Cleave in which he generalizes my proposal for defining logical
validity of sentences with inexact predicates and demonstrates the
technical viability of the generalized definition (see note 1 on p. 81).

Chapter I

In its common use the term 'category' simply means a class, usually a fairly comprehensive class, of entities. The technical refinements of this use proposed by Aristotle, Kant and other philosophers are so heterogeneous that none of them can be regarded as firmly established. In these circumstances the introduction of the term 'categorial framework' in a technical sense needs no excuse, particularly if it respects some of the older uses of its cognates and serves similar ends. It is the main task of this chapter to define and to expound this notion.

The steps leading to the definition of a categorial framework are first, a discussion of the classification of all entities with special emphasis on the difference between arbitrary classes and natural kinds; second, a preliminary examination of the relations holding, on the one hand, between the 'categories' or maximal kinds of a natural classification and, on the other hand, between the maximal kinds and their subordinate genera; third, a general characterization of the attributes the joint possession of which is a necessary and sufficient condition of an entity's being a member of a maximal kind, and of the attributes the joint possession of which is a necessary and sufficient condition of an entity's being a distinct, individual member of a maximal kind; fourth, a discussion of the logical assumptions involved in the categorization of all entities into maximal kinds and of the constitution and individuation of their members. The chapter will be concluded by distinguishing our 'ontological' sense of categorization from other senses especially a 'syntactical' and 'semantical' sense of the term and by guarding the notion of a categorial framework against other misunderstandings.

Natural classifications

All thinking involves classification and every classification involves judgments to the effect that one or more objects possess, or lack, one or more characteristics. The notions of an object and of a characteristic cannot be defined independently. An object is what possesses characteristics; a characteristic is what is actually or, as in the case of 'omniscient', at least conceivably possessed by an object. Since characteristics in turn possess characteristics, they are also objects. But not all objects are characteristics. Whether or not an object is a characteristic is not always clear or generally agreed. Thus the words 'Napoleon Bonaparte' refer in the view of most people to an object which is not a characteristic or a combination of characteristics. But as regards that which is referred to by 'the number two', the situation is much less uniform. Some regard it as a characteristic (of classes, aggregates, or patterns), others as an object which is not a characteristic, still others are not committed to either view.

Psychology, anthropology, and comparative linguistics bear witness to the variety of ways in which different persons and groups of persons differentiate the world or experience into objects. Yet whatever the objects which a person discerns or is capable of discerning, their totality may be classified in more ways than one. Let us call a classification of all objects discerned or discernible by a person a total classification if it satisfies the following conditions: (a) all objects are classified into a finite set of non-empty classes, say $\alpha_1 \ldots \alpha_n$ such that—apart from common borderline cases—any two classes are exclusive of each other; (b) the objects belonging to each of these classes are again classified in the same manner; (c) the process of subclassification is repeated a finite number of times.

A classification may strike one as more or less natural; and a classification which seems natural to some people may seem wholly unnatural to others. Consider, for example, a total classification which at its highest level comprises a class to which belong all men, all colours, all prime numbers and nothing else. It may be possible to imagine a society to whose way of life the distinction between this class and all others is so important that no classification would appear natural to any member of the society unless it contained this class at the highest classificatory level. Yet to anybody brought up in any Western tradition such a classification would appear quite unnatural.

Why is this so? To say that a natural classification must respect natural differences is no answer. But if one considers (as far as one can see) the great variety of classifications which have been used at one time or another one is led to formulate three types of distinction which, in the eyes of its users, a natural classification respects at least to some extent: (i) It distinguishes between objects which are and objects which are not 'logically ultimate', i.e. objects which are the possessors of characteristics but are not themselves characteristics and objects which are both possessors of characteristics and characteristics. (ii) It distinguishes between objects which are and objects which are not 'ontologically fundamental', i.e. objects which exist apart from and independently of other objects and objects which do not so exist. (iii) It distinguishes between objects which are 'psychologically co-ordinate', i.e. belong together, and objects which are 'psychologically disparate', i.e. do not belong together. These distinctions, which may be called 'logical', 'ontological', and 'psychological', though still vague, are of some use in explaining the difference between natural and unnatural classifications. We reject a total classification of the sort mentioned in the example because it is wholly alien is our way of drawing these logical, ontological, and psychological distinctions.

The logical and ontological distinctions—or, to avoid exegetic controversy, very similar ones—were explicitly made by Aristotle.[1] He defines (primary) substances as logically ultimate and ontologically fundamental objects. 'Substance in the truest and strictest sense of the term', he says, 'is that which can be neither asserted of nor found in the subject.' His examples of (primary) substances are a particular man or a particular horse. His counterexamples include attributes, which are not logically ultimate, and colours, which he does not regard as ontologically fundamental. Aristotle does not examine or even consider the possibility of a natural classification in which particular men or horses are not ontologically fundamental, but dependent for their existence on the existence of objects for which his own classificatory scheme has made no provision. He holds that *his* distinction between substances and non-substances is absolute and (it seems) holds the even stronger view that in the nature of things and of thought there can be only one truly natural classification.

If the ontological distinction is less precise than the logical one, the psychological distinction is much more vague than either. Yet it is possible to discern some general principles by which degrees of co-ordination and disparateness between objects are determined. Thus, as has been pointed out by the British empiricists,[2] objects of commonsense thinking are often grouped together if they resemble each other in one or more respects, if they are near each other in space and time, if they are traceable to a common cause of their existence, etc. Objects of theoretical thinking are often grouped together if they are isomorphic, if they are produced by the same recursive process, if they are within certain contexts identifiable with the same objects of commonsense thinking, etc. Apart from these and similar principles of co-ordination and disparity, the grouping of objects into natural classes depends on personal and social attitudes, interests, and purposes. Traditional distinctions between artificial and natural classes find their expression in natural languages in which simpler locutions tend to be reserved for natural classes. If our lives would so change that the artificial class consisting of all men, all colours, all prime numbers and nothing else became a natural class, we should probably come to use one word for any member of it.

[1] See esp. *Categoriae*, ch. V (Bekker, 2a 11).
[2] See, e.g., Hume's *A Treatise of Human Nature*, Book I, Section IV.

Categorizations

It seems reasonable to expect that a person's metaphysical convictions and standards of intelligibility are intimately related to his conception of a natural, as opposed to an artificial, total classification. It seems no less reasonable to expect that the nature of this relation will be more clearly expressed in the higher and more abstract levels of a total classification than in the lower and more concrete ones. It will be convenient to reserve the term 'categorization' for the higher levels of a total classification and to define it in a special sense which is yet rooted in philosophical tradition. A categorization in this sense consists of the following phases each of which represents an acknowledged or rejected natural partition, i.e. the division of all objects or of all objects of a natural class into two or more *non-empty*, jointly exhaustive, and (apart from possible common borderline cases) mutually exclusive natural classes.

The phases are: (i) Acknowledgment of a partition of all objects into (a) a class of particulars, i.e. objects which are logically ultimate and (b) a class of attributes, i.e. objects which are not logically ultimate. (ii) *Either* acknowledgment of a partition of all particulars into (a) a class of independent particulars, i.e. particulars which are ontologically fundamental and (b) a class of dependent particulars, i.e. particulars which are not ontologically fundamental; *or* rejection of such a partition because one of the classes is empty. (iii) *Either* acknowledgment of a partition of all attributes into (a) a class of independent attributes or universals, i.e. attributes which are ontologically fundamental and (b) a class of dependent attributes, i.e. attributes which are not ontologically fundamental; *or* rejection of such a partition because one of the classes is empty. (iv) If the class of independent particulars is not empty, then *either* acknowledgment of a partition of this class into two or more maximal classes of independent particulars *or* rejection of such a partition as unnatural (e.g. because there exists only one independent particular). (v) If the class of dependent particulars is not empty, then *either* acknowledgment of a partition of this class into two or more maximal classes of dependent particulars *or* rejection of such a partition as unnatural. Lastly, (vi) and (vii) which read respectively like (iv) and (v) with 'attribute' taking the place of 'particular'.

Before commenting on various types of categorization it will be useful to draw attention to some of the traditional roots of our notion of categorization. As regards (i), the partition of all objects into particulars and attributes is generally acknowledged. The clearest modern version of it is probably that of Frege.[1] As regards (ii), the partition of all

---

[1] See 'Über Begriff und Gegenstand', *Vierteljahrschrift für wissenschaftliche Philosophie* **16** (1892). [See *Translations from the Philosophical Writings of Gottlob Frege* by Geach and Black, 2nd edition (Oxford, 1960).]

bottom-layer (chapter IV). For the moment, however, we shall simply consider maximal kinds of particulars—quite apart from the question whether they are independent or dependent.

A person may be able to classify a particular as a member of a certain maximal kind or to identify it as a distinct individual member of this kind without being able to formulate any clear principle by which the classification or identification is made. His inability to do so may be due to the absence of such a principle because the maximal kind itself is not clearly demarcated. Frequently, however, these instinctive classifications and identifications can be made more explicit, especially by indicating (a) attributes which characterize a particular as a member of a maximal kind and (b) attributes which characterize a particular which is a member of a maximal kind as a distinct, individual member of it. In accordance with traditional usage—or at least without grossly violating it—the former attributes will be called 'constitutive' and the latter 'individuating'.

More precisely, I shall say that an attribute, say C_1, is constitutive of the particulars of a maximal kind, say M, if and only if (i) the attribute is applicable to some particulars, i.e. C_1 is not empty; and (ii) the particular's belonging to the maximal kind logically implies the applicability of the attribute to the particular, i.e. 'being an M' logically implies 'being a C_1'. (If $C_1 \ldots C_n$ are constitutive of M and of no other maximal kind, then 'being an M' not only logically implies but is also logically implied by 'being a C_1 and $\ldots$ and a C_n'.) I shall say that a proposition is a constitutive principle associated with a maximal kind, if to assert the proposition is to assert that a certain attribute, say C_1, is constitutive of the particulars of a certain maximal kind, say M.

I shall say that an attribute, say D, is individuating for the particulars of a maximal kind, say M, if and only if (i) D is not empty; and (ii) for every particular belonging to M there is available a subattribute S of D (S is not empty, 'being an S' logically implies 'being a D') such that a particular's belonging to M and possessing S logically implies, and is logically implied by, the particular's being a distinct instance of M, briefly 'being an M and an S' logically implies, and is logically implied by, 'being a distinct M'. I shall say that a proposition is an individuating principle associated with a maximal kind, if to assert the proposition is to assert that a certain attribute, say D, is individuating for the particulars of a certain maximal kind, say, M.

The notion of logical implication used in the definitions of constitutive and individuating attributes and of constitutive and individuating principles requires and will presently be subjected to analysis. Before doing so, however, it will be useful to exemplify the newly defined notions and to indicate their ancestry. Consider the familiar example of a person who acknowledges the class of physical objects as a maximal

2

kind and whose common sense thinking about the class of particulars has been directly or indirectly influenced by Newtonian physics or a philosophy inspired by it. For such a person the attribute 'x stands in a causal relation to y' with x and y ranging over physical objects (and perhaps other objects too) is constitutive of the particulars belonging to the class of physical objects. For him (i) 'x stands in a causal relation to y' is not empty and (ii) 'Being a physical object' logically implies 'standing in a causal relation to some other physical (and perhaps other) object'. The principle of causality, namely that every physical object stands in a causal relation of the kind mentioned or, to put it differently, that the causal relation is constitutive of all physical objects, is for him a constitutive principle associated with the maximal kind of physical objects.

The person in our example would further employ the attribute $D =$ 'x is located in absolute, Euclidean, three-dimensional space and in absolute time' as individuating for all physical objects. The sub-attribute S by the possession of which a physical object is distinguished from all others is its location in a specific path through absolute space and time. For the person (i) D is not empty and (ii) 'being a physical object and an S' logically implies, and is logically implied by 'being a distinct physical object'. And the principle that D is individuating for all physical objects is for him the individuating principle associated with the maximal kind of physical objects.

Our definition of the terms 'constitutive' and 'individuating' as qualifying attributes and principles is etymologically sound and in line with ordinary usage. It is also well anchored in philosophical tradition. The former is used by Kant in a sense which is similar to ours, except that he does not consider the possibility of alternative categorizations and of alternative constitutive principles. The latter term occurs traditionally mainly in attempts to answer the question as to what makes any object—rather than an object of a certain kind—a distinct individual object.

Categorization and logic

To categorize all objects into maximal kinds is—explicitly or implicitly—to apply a notion of logical implication. A person who acknowledges, say, M_1 and M_2 as maximal kinds holds that (apart from possible common borderline cases) being a member of M_1 logically implies not being a member of M_2. That acknowledging a constitutive or individuating principle involves acknowledging a logical implication is obvious since any such principle is a conjunction of an existential proposition and a logical implication.

Logical or, more precisely, logically valid implications are merely one kind of logical propositions. For just as there are logically valid and not logically valid implications, so there are also, for example, logically valid and not logically valid disjunctions. The logical validity or otherwise of a proposition is determined by reference to a logic, that is to say a set of (logical) principles to the effect that any proposition possessing certain formal or structural characteristics is true whatever its other features may be. The logics to be considered in the following chapters are a version of classical logic L, so called after the logicists who gave it its modern form; and a version of constructive logic I, so called after the intuitionists who first made explicit use of it. In addition to L and I, I shall also consider the extensions L^* and I^* of these systems (in order to allow for logical relations not only between 'exact' propositions but also between exact and 'inexact' propositions and between inexact propositions). In both of these systems the formal or structural features characterizing its logically valid propositions are unambiguously defined in terms of (standardized formulae expressing) 'propositional forms' and their 'substitution-instances'. But the definitions differ from one logical system to another.

Roughly speaking, a propositional form differs from a proposition in that one or more of its distinct constituent propositions, attributes or particulars are replaced by distinct variables ranging respectively over propositions, attributes or particulars. A substitution-instance of a propositional form is a proposition derived from it by substituting distinct constants for the corresponding distinct variables. (For example, 'John is taller than Charles' is a substitution-instance of 'xRy' of which another substitution-instance is 'Bristol is south-west of London'.) It will, for the moment, be enough to exemplify the differences between logical validity in the mentioned logical systems by two assertions, which will be justified in due course. First, whereas in L every substitution-instance of 'p or not-p' is a logically valid proposition, this is not the case in I, L^* or I^*. Second, whereas L and I contain propositional forms all of whose substitution-instances are logically valid propositions, L^* and I^*, do not contain such propositional forms. The validity of the propositions of L^* and I^* is defined in terms of valid forms of L and I.[1]

The actual, and possible, multiplicity of categorizations and of constitutive and individuating principles associated with the maximal kinds of a categorization is thus matched by a multiplicity of logics with respect to which the logical validity of implications and other propositions is determined. If a person in employing a categorial framework F determines the logical validity or otherwise of the propositions which he believes—in particular of the implications assumed in formulating

[1] For details about L, L^* and I, I^* see chs. III and IV and the Appendix, where two further systems A (Ackermann's system of rigorous implication) and A^* are also considered.

his categorization, his constitutive and individuating principles—by reference to a logical system say L, then L is part of F and will be called the 'logic underlying F'. It is, as we shall see, quite feasible that a person should apart from this 'primary logic' also employ another logic in a secondary or auxiliary manner.

Apart from problems concerning the analysis of all logically valid propositions, there are some concerning only logical implication. One of these is the question about the distinction between logical implications which are and logical implications which are not 'paradoxical'. In so far as the notion of a paradoxical or apparently paradoxical logical implication admits of a structural characterization, it has been taken to comprise (a) some, if not all, logical implications with a logically impossible antecedent, e.g. (writing '$\Rightarrow$' for 'logically implies') (p and $not\text{-}p$) $\Rightarrow q$; (b) some, if not all, logical implications with a logically necessary consequent, e.g. $p \Rightarrow not(q$ and $not\text{-}q)$; (c) some, if not all logical, implications in which the number of implication-signs in the antecedent and in the consequent is unequal, e.g. $p \Rightarrow (q \Rightarrow p)$. All the logical systems considered (in the text) will admit 'paradoxical' implications. However, the logical implications which are asserted in the formulation of categorizations, of constitutive and of individuating principles are not paradoxical in the sense of (a)–(c). For none of them contains a logically impossible antecedent, a logically necessary consequent or an unequal number of '$\Rightarrow$' in antecedent and consequent.

The notion of a categorial framework

By drawing together the results of the preceding discussion it is possible to define the useful notion of a categorial framework. To indicate a thinker's categorial framework is to make explicit (i) his categorization of objects, (ii) the constitutive and individuating principles associated with the maximal kinds of his categorization, (iii) the logic underlying his thinking.

The notion of a categorial framework, as defined here, does not prejudge the question whether there is or is not only one true, correct, or wholly adequate categorial framework. In this respect it differs from the Aristotelian, Kantian, and Fregean notions of which it is a partial amalgam. If, as these and many other philosophers hold, there is only one true categorial framework and if, moreover, this framework can be established only by a specifically philosophical method, then philosophy becomes the ultimate court of appeal in judging the adequacy of all thinking in so far as it depends on its categorial framework. It becomes, for example, the final judge of the categorizations, categorial principles, and underlying logic employed in the natural sciences and mathematics.

If no one categorial framework can be singled out as true, correct, or wholly adequate, then the philosophers' concern with categorial frameworks may still be peculiar to philosophy without being spurious. It is in particular plausible to assume that metaphysicians who appeared to themselves and to others to be engaged in establishing the true categorial framework were in fact doing something else. They were exhibiting or modifying the categorial frameworks employed by them and their con- temporaries, making speculative proposals of radically new categorial frameworks and justifying either the categorial *status quo* or categorial change. But in that case philosophy cannot claim to be the final judge of the adequacy of any categorial framework or the thinking which proceeds within it. If, for example, a new scientific theory violates an established categorial framework, it is by no means 'philosophically' obvious whether the theory should be adjusted to the framework or the framework to the theory. (See chapter VI.)

Ontological as distinct from semantic classifications

Ontological categorizations, which are classifications of all objects discernible by a thinker, differ from grammatical categorizations, i.e. classifications of the parts of a language or the corresponding speech, and from semantic categorizations, i.e. classifications of the meaningful parts of a language or the corresponding speech. The objects of grammar and semantics are only a subclass of the objects of ontology. Nothing is gained if one blurs this distinction by speaking vaguely of philosophical grammar and philosophical semantics. Nevertheless since that which can be talked about in a language includes what is believed by its speakers to exist, the grammar and semantics of a language are useful in discovering the ontological assumptions of its speakers. A few remarks about the limited usefulness of dictionaries in discovering the onto- logical commitments of the speakers of a language will here have to take the place of a more systematic inquiry into the relations between ontology on the one hand and grammar and semantics on the other.

The speakers of the same language may and usually do differ in their classifications—even on the highest classificatory levels. Thus a diction- ary of the English language, even though it may acknowledge in principle the distinction between particulars and attributes, is not a reliable guide to the actual distinctions made by all speakers of English. Thus the Concise Oxford Dictionary will not help us in discovering which of them regard the number two as a particular and which of them as an attribute. Its definition of 'number' as 'tale, count, sum, company or aggregate of persons . . . or things . . . or abstract units' suggests that its compilers regarded numbers as complex particulars, but does not commit other speakers of English to the same ontological assumption.

Again, a dictionary is not necessarily a reliable guide to the division, if any, between independent and dependent particulars made in the categorizations of the speakers of the language. The commonsense, for example, which is reflected by the Concise Oxford Dictionary involves the assumption that some particulars cannot exist apart from or independently of others. Yet this assumption is compatible both with acknowledging and with rejecting any specific division of the class of particulars into a class of independent and a class of dependent ones. Such an acknowledgment or rejection becomes for many people explicit only after examining that area of their enlightened commonsense which is most open to the sectarian influences of philosophical and scientific fashions. It is in any case unlikely that a dictionary could reflect all divisions made by the past, present, and future speakers of a language dividing the particulars and attributes acknowledged by them into independent and dependent ones.

Although dictionaries are intended to convey 'meanings' rather than 'factual information' they are not free from existence-assumptions. The compiler of any dictionary assumes that there are objects, that some of them are particulars and that others are attributes. His subclassification of the class of particulars into maximal kinds of (independent or dependent) particulars must contain at least one class which is not empty. But if he distinguishes between two or more maximal classes he may leave open the question which of these classes are and which of them are not empty; and a classification of particulars into classes, some of which may be empty, does not reflect a division of particulars into (non-empty) maximal kinds. For example, the entry in the Concise Oxford Dictionary which describes a seraph as a celestial being does not imply that all or some speakers of current English employ a categorization which acknowledges a class of celestial beings as one of its maximal kinds of (independent or dependent) particulars. In order to find out which speakers acknowledge this maximal kind an empirical inquiry is needed which goes beyond the empirical inquiry directed towards the discovery of 'semantic categories', i.e. possibly empty maximal classes.

Before engaging in a more detailed examination of the structure and function of categorial frameworks, it might be advisable to offer some conciliatory replies to certain sweeping objections which, if justified, would cast serious doubt on our whole enterprise. The first objection is that nobody employs a categorial framework. The objection would be justified if 'to employ a categorial framework' meant to be explicitly and continually aware of the distinctions and assumptions to which the term 'categorial framework' refers. But I no more make this absurd claim than did the philosophers who first investigated the categories and structure of thinking. I am, moreover, prepared to admit that some people's ontological commitments are—at some or all periods of their lives—less definite than my definitions seem to imply. Thus a definite distinction between independent and dependent particulars or a definite commitment to a specific individuating principle associated with a specific maximal kind may be lacking or at least be inaccessible to the most careful reflection, questioning, or other empirical techniques. A reader who regards my statements as sharper and stronger than warranted by the facts should find it easy to render them less sharp and less strong.

The second objection is that everybody employs more than one categorial framework. The objection would be justified if 'to employ a categorial framework' meant to employ one and only one categorial framework throughout one's life. But I do not wish to deny the possibility of categorial change and shall (in chapter VI) inquire into some aspects of it. I am moreover prepared to admit that a person may at times waver in his commitment to one categorial framework rather than another.

The third objection is that, even if every human being has up to now employed a categorial framework (or made the kind of distinctions and assumptions to which the term refers), it is possible that future generations will be able to think or, if we prefer, to apprehend the world without employing any categorial framework. To assert this possibility as an objection to anything I have so far said or shall say in later chapters rests on a misunderstanding, since I nowhere deny this possibility.

Chapter II

While the possibility of apprehending the world without employing any categorial framework, for example through mystical experiences, will not concern us here, we shall examine the possibility of different categorial frameworks being employed by different people. Because of a natural inclination to elevate the peculiarities of one's own thinking into universal characteristics of all rational thought, philosophers tend to regard categorial frameworks as only apparently different and as reducible to a common standard type. If we are to avoid the distortions resulting from this point of view we must try to understand the sense in which, and the extent to which, the propositions and distinctions which are characteristic of a categorial framework are incorrigible if viewed from the inside and corrigible if viewed from the outside of it.

In the present chapter I shall explain the difference between externally and internally incorrigible propositions, examine the special cases of internally incorrigible existential and of internally incorrigible logical propositions and show that the constitutive and individuating principles associated with a categorial framework are each a conjunction of an internally, but not externally, incorrigible existential and an internally, but not externally, incorrigible logical proposition. I shall then examine the internally, but not externally, incorrigible distinctions between independent and dependent particulars and between primary and secondary logical systems. In conclusion I shall compare and contrast the notions of internal and external incorrigibility with the notion of truth. When appropriate, I shall compare some of the newly defined relative concepts with their traditional absolute counterparts.

On internally incorrigible propositions

A proposition g is, roughly speaking, incorrigible with respect to a categorial framework F if, and only if, to reject g is *eo ipso* to abandon F. To be more precise, let f be the conjunction of the propositions which together characterize F, that is to say (i) the propositions which express the categorization of F; (ii) the constitutive principles associated with the maximal kinds of F; (iii) the individuating principles associated with the maximal kinds of F; (iv) the principles of the logic underlying F.

Thus a proposition g is incorrigible with respect to F if, and only if, f logically—that is, in accordance with the logic underlying F—implies g. If, as is customary, we write '$\vdash_S$' for 'logically implies in accordance with the logical system S underlying F', the incorrigibility of g with respect to S can be expressed concisely by: $f \vdash_S g$, or still more concisely by $f \vdash g$. In contexts which leave no doubt about the framework with respect to which a proposition is incorrigible, I shall often say simply that the proposition is internally incorrigible.

In order to exemplify the notion of internal incorrigibility, we may again consider a member of the family of categorial frameworks employed by those of our contemporaries whose thinking has been moulded by pre-twentieth-century science and a philosophy accepting its results. We may, moreover, so choose our examples that the differences between the members of the family can be neglected. To a person employing any one of these categorial frameworks, say F_0, the propositions which are incorrigible with respect to it will comprise: (i) the proposition that dogs have no immortal souls (because whether or not the class of organisms with immortal souls is, or is included in, a maximal kind of F_0 it does not comprise any dogs); (ii) the proposition that all natural events are governed by immutable laws of nature (because the proposition is logically implied by the principle of causality which is one of the constitutive principles associated with a maximal kind of F_0); (iii) the proposition that time is one-dimensional (because the proposition is logically implied by those individuating principles of F_0 which refer to temporal relations); (iv) the proposition that every proposition is either true or false (because the proposition is a principle of the logic underlying F_0—irrespective of whether in a given formulation of this logic it is an axiom, or a theorem).

It is important to distinguish the internal incorrigibility of a proposition, i.e. its incorrigibility with respect to a specific categorial framework, from its external incorrigibility, i.e. its incorrigibility with respect to any categorial framework which has been, or might be, employed. In order to show that a proposition g_0 which is incorrigible with respect to one categorial framework, say F_1, is not externally incorrigible one has to present another categorial framework, say F_2, such that g_0 is not incorrigible with respect to F_2. One simply has to show that whereas it is the case that $f_1 \vdash_S g_0$ it is *not* the case that $f_2 \vdash_S g_0$. For example, if 'g_0' stands for 'Dogs have immortal souls'; f_1 contains the constitutive principle that being a member of the class of animals, conceived as a maximal kind, logically implies having an immortal soul; and f_2 does not logically imply that there are immortal souls; then $f_1 \vdash_S g_0$ whereas *not* $(f_2 \vdash_S g_0)$ so that 'Dogs have immortal souls' is incorrigible with respect to F_1 but not with respect to F_2.

Our example has been constructed on the tacit assumption that F_1

and F_2 have the same underlying logic. But it may well be that this is not so and that whereas the logic underlying F_1 is S, the logic underlying F_2 is, say, T. In that case it may, as before, be that f_1 S-logically (in accordance with the logic S) implies g_0 and that f_2 does *not* S-logically imply g_0. But the reason for the absence of the S-logical implication—i.e. for *not* $(f_2 \vdash_S g_0)$—is the trivial one that, in accordance with f_2, no S-implication whatever is available not only between f_2 and g_0 but between any propositions capable of being accommodated in F_2. If in accordance with f_2 only statements of T-implications are valid, then no statement of an S-implication can be valid in accordance with f_2.

If the relation between the logical systems S and T is well understood, it may be possible to indicate precisely the manner in which, as a result of replacing S by T, a non-logical proposition whose logical relations to other propositions is determined by S is transformed into a non-logical proposition whose logical relations to other propositions is determined by T. Let us, for the moment, write F^S and F^T for two categorial frameworks with underlying logic S and T respectively such that the first is transformed into the second by replacing S by T and *vice versa*; let us write f^S and f^T for the conjunctions which respectively describe the two frameworks; and lastly let us write g_0^S and g_0^T for two non-logical propositions transformable into each other by replacing S by T or *vice versa*. We can then define a strong notion of internal incorrigibility which takes these transformations into account: A non-logical proposition g_0^S is incorrigible with respect to F^S *and* F^T if, and only if, $f^S \vdash_S g_0^S$ and $f^T \vdash_T g_0^T$. (Thus, if we assume that in our last example F_2 results from F_1 through replacing L by I and *vice versa* then, if 'Dogs have immortal souls' is incorrigible with respect to F_1 its transform would also be incorrigible with respect to F_2 and *vice versa*.)

One is sometimes in the position of comparing two categorial frameworks whose relations to each other are quite transparent, so that even though one employs one of them, one understands clearly what it would be like to employ the other. That this is not always the case will be admitted by anybody who alone, or with the help of experts, has tried to understand the thought of an unfamiliar culture—expressed in a familiar or unfamiliar language. When it comes to comparing imperfectly understood categorial frameworks with our own or with each other, we often lack the criteria for deciding whether or not, say, g_0 as referred to F and g_0^1 as referred to F^1 are 'the same proposition', 'logical transforms of each other' or otherwise 'equivalent'. However, the problem of comparison in these circumstances is best postponed until the general structure of categorial frameworks has been examined in some detail. See (Chapter VI, p. 63f.)

On internally incorrigible existential and logical propositions

The concepts of internal and external incorrigibility have useful applica- tions within and, one would expect, outside philosophy. By applying them to existential and logical propositions one arrives at a better understanding of the structure and function of categorial frameworks, since the description of any categorial framework involves existential and logical propositions. Among other things it also becomes possible to purge some traditional and deeply rooted doctrines about the 'a priori' character of all 'analytic'—or of all 'analytic' and some 'syn- thetic'—propositions of confusion and error while preserving what is valuable in these doctrines.

By an existential proposition I shall understand any proposition to the effect that one or more particulars of a certain kind exist and any proposition which logically implies an existential proposition. A con- junction of an existential and a non-existential proposition is thus existential. As regards the relation between existential propositions and a categorial framework F we may distinguish between existential propositions which are and those which are not existential with respect to F; and among those which are existential with respect to F between those which are and those which are not incorrigibly existential with respect to F.

More precisely, an existential proposition g is existential with respect to a categorial framework F if, and only if, it is consistent with the proposition that no maximal kind of F is empty and that every particular belongs to one of them. This proposition, which is of course contained in f—the conjunction describing F—might be called the 'basic existential thesis' of F. A proposition which is existential with respect to F is incorrigibly existential with respect to F if, and only if, it is not only consistent with the basic existential thesis of F, but logically implied by the thesis—and therefore by f. Thus if $M_1 \ldots M_n$ are the maximal kinds of F then g is incorrigibly existential with respect to F if, and only if, it is logically implied by the proposition that $M_1 \ldots M_n$ between them comprise all particulars and that none of them is empty.

It may be that a proposition which is existential with respect to one categorial framework is not existential with respect to another; that a proposition which is existential with respect to a framework is not incorrigibly existential with respect to it; and that a proposition which is incorrigibly existential with respect to one categorial framework is not incorrigibly existential, or even existential, with respect to another. Assume, for example, that F acknowledges the class of material objects as a maximal kind but regards the class of spirits as empty; and that F' acknowledges the class of spirits as a maximal kind, but regards the class of material objects as empty. The proposition 'I saw a dog', provided that dogs are conceived as material objects, will then be existential with respect to F but not with respect to F'. And it will not be incorrigibly existential with respect to F. The proposition that there are material objects and the proposition that whatever particular may exist, it is not a spirit, are incorrigibly existential with respect to F and not even existential with respect to F'.

In explaining the general notion of a categorial framework and of its underlying logic, I have emphasized the possibility of different underlying logics and mentioned those logical systems which will come under more detailed discussion. If S is the logic underlying F then the logical propositions which are incorrigible with respect to F are (i) the logical principles of S which characterize the logically valid propositions of S in terms of propositional forms and their substitution instances; and (ii) the logically valid propositions themselves. (The S-logical consequences of (i) and (ii) are already included under (i) and (ii).)

While it might be readily agreed that some logical propositions are incorrigible with respect to all categorial frameworks with one underlying logic, but not with respect to any categorial framework with another underlying logic, it may yet seem that there are also logical propositions which are incorrigible with respect to any categorial framework, whatever its underlying logic. An example of the first kind would be the proposition g_0 or not-g_0, which is a substitution instance of the form g or not-g.[1] The proposition, it would be agreed, is valid in L, i.e. classical logic, but not in I, i.e. intuitionist logic. An example of the second kind would be the proposition not (g_0 and not-g_0), which is a substitution instance of the form not (g and not-g). The proposition, it might be said, is valid in every logic and, therefore, a fortiori in both L and I because it represents an application of the law of contradiction.

This view does not stand up to closer examination. Since not (g_0 and not-g_0) L-logically implies g_0 or not-g_0, but does not I-logically imply g_0 or not-g_0, the expression 'not (g_0 and not-g_0)' represents two nonequivalent propositions, i.e. two propositions which do not I- or L-logically imply each other. But then the statement that the proposition not (g_0 and not-g_0) is logically valid in L and in I is either false or an elliptical way of stating that of the two different propositions represented by 'not (g_0 and not-g_0)' in L and I respectively, the first is valid in L and the second is valid in I. If the view that the one proposition not (g_0 and not-g_0) is valid in L and I, and thus incorrigible with respect to any categorial framework with underlying L or I, breaks down because there is no one such proposition, it follows that there is no one logical proposition not (g_0 and not-g_0) which is incorrigible with respect to every categorial framework, i.e. externally incorrigible.

[1] Wherever constants are contrasted with variables the constants will normally be written with subscripts and the variables without subscripts.

Similar remarks apply to logical equivalence by—or based on—definition. If in any of the logical systems under consideration, say L, an expression 'g' representing a proposition stands by definition for an expression 'h', then g L-logically implies, and is L-logically implied by, h. This bilateral, L-logical implication must, like any other, be distinguished from, say, a bilateral I-logical implication. (Because not-not-g L-logically implies g, we may from this L-logical and our bilateral L-logical implication deduce that not-not-h L-logically implies g. The analogous deduction in I is not valid because not-not-g does not I-logically imply g.)

The notions of internally incorrigible, internally incorrigible existential and internally incorrigible logical propositions are to some extent relativized versions of Kant's *a priori, a priori* synthetic and *a priori* analytic propositions. There is no need to justify this statement by any detailed exegesis of Kant's works, especially as the reasons for defining and using the relative notions have nothing to do with the question of their genuine or apparent absolute ancestry. It is sufficient to note that the propositions which in the *Critique of Pure Reason* are characterized as *a priori*, as analytic (and, therefore, *a priori*), and as synthetic *a priori* correspond respectively to our internally incorrigible, our internally incorrigible logical and our internally incorrigible existential propositions. In particular, the Kantian principles of the individuation and constitution of external phenomena—by their spatio-temporal location in Euclidean space and time and by the applicability to them of the twelve Categories—are internally incorrigible existential propositions. More precisely they are, like all individuating and constitutive principles, each a conjunction of an internally incorrigible existential and an internally incorrigible logical proposition, and thus an internally incorrigible existential proposition.

On internally incorrigible distinctions between independent and dependent particulars

From the internal incorrigibilities which derive from the existential assumptions of a categorial framework and its underlying logic I turn to internally incorrigible distinctions between independent and dependent particulars. For reasons which are not far to seek, some, if not all, of these distinctions seem less deeply rooted in our thinking. Thus it is possible to think effectively about particulars and relations between particulars without any awareness of any clear distinction between independent and dependent particulars. Indeed for many ordinary purposes no such distinction is needed. No similar detachment can be maintained about the question whether a class of particulars is a maximal kind and thus not empty or which propositions follow from which. Again, if one has made a distinction between independent and dependent particulars, one may modify it without changing one's classification into maximal kinds by simply 'promoting' a dependent to an independent maximal kind or *vice versa*. An example would be a change of mind by a philosopher or a physicist who has hitherto regarded space (or space–time) as merely a set of relations between physical objects and thus dependent for its existence on the existence of physical objects; and who now regards physical objects as geometro-dynamical manifestations of space (or space–time).[1]

Because the internally incorrigible existential assumptions and logical principles of a categorial framework are rarely questioned and do not obviously admit of alternatives, it was advisable, or at least excusable, to show at some length that their internal incorrigibility does not imply their external incorrigibility. There is no similar reluctance to question distinctions between independent and dependent particulars and no scarcity of alternative proposals. And there is in any case no need to repeat the previous argument with obvious minor modifications. Its up-shot is that, whereas by rejecting such a distinction one *ipso facto* rejects any categorial framework of which it is characteristic, it does by no means follow that there is or can be no categorial framework which does not contain the distinction.

Most metaphysicians follow Aristotle not only in distinguishing be-tween independent and dependent particulars, but also in holding that their own distinction is absolute. The arguments in support of this particular uniqueness claim are (not particularly interesting) special cases of more general types of inconclusive or wholly fallacious argu-ments, some of which will be examined in due course (chapter VI). But they are often rounded off by an alleged explanation which is supposed to show the propounder of the rejected distinction as having fallen victim to a linguistic confusion of autosemantic (categorematic) and synsemantic (syncategorematic) symbols. Here autosemantic symbols are understood as referring singly or distributively to independent particulars, whereas synsemantic symbols function merely as parts of autosemantic symbols. The confusion arises when a synsemantic symbol, which looks like an autosemantic symbol, is taken for such.

For example, let us assume that I acknowledge only the classes of material objects and of angels as maximal kinds of independent parti-culars and that you—perhaps without being clearly aware of this—do likewise. If you nevertheless tell me that thoughts are independent particulars, I may make you see the errors of your ontological ways by arguing that whereas 'a man having a thought' or 'an angel having a thought' are autosemantic symbols, 'thought' is a synsemantic symbol which looks like an autosemantic one merely because of the accidents of grammar. It is worth noting that in so arguing I should be imitating—

---

[1] See, e.g., J. A. Wheeler *Geometrodynamics* (New York and London, 1962).

albeit somewhat crudely—a famous argument by Brentano.[1] But the force of any such argument based on a specific distinction between auto-semantic and synsemantic symbols presupposes our prior adoption of the corresponding ontological distinction between independent and dependent particulars. The linguistic distinction implements or exhibits a prior ontological distinction. It neither enforces nor justifies its adoption.

On internally incorrigible distinctions between primary and secondary logical systems

A distinction between maximal kinds and, more particularly, between independent and dependent maximal kinds does not by itself imply a difference in the structure of reasoning about the members of the distinguished kinds. Thus the rules to which we conform in our reasoning about physical objects and regions of space are unaffected by our assumption that physical objects are independent particulars and that space is a dependent particular, and remain unaffected if we undergo a conversion to the opposite metaphysical conviction. Two maximal kinds of the same categorial framework may, however, differ from each other not only in their members, but in the manner of reasoning which is, or is taken to be, appropriate to them. In that case there may arise the ontological question as to which, if any, of the two modes of reasoning is the primary logical system, underlying the categorial framework, and which is merely auxiliary or secondary.

Aristotle, whose absolute distinction between independent and dependent particulars has to be relativized, does not consider an absolute distinction between primary and secondary logic. To consider its very possibility presupposes some explicit awareness of at least two serious competitors for ontological supremacy—an awareness which has emerged only fairly recently after the development of an autonomous intuitionist mathematics. Only when one could point to the fact that the intuitionists employ a non-classical logic in their reasoning about mathematical entities, did it appear reasonable to ask whether this logic was primary; and if so whether it was primary with respect to every categorial framework or with respect to some categorial frameworks but not to others. To the uncommitted the ensuing metaphysical battle about the ontological primacy of intuitionist logic may, like the older wars of ontological independence of this or that maximal kind, appear wasteful and even futile. Yet this battle has led to insights which are of value also to a non-combatant. One of them is the recognition that in employing a categorial framework one may, apart from its underlying or primary logic, also use a secondary logical theory.

---

[1] See, e.g., *Die Lehre vom richtigen Urteil* (edited by F. Mayer-Hillebrand, Bern, 1956). §§16 ff.

It will be the task of the next two chapters to distinguish between the subject matter and logical structure of constructive thinking on the one hand and of factual thinking on the other, and to examine their inter-relation (chapter III); and similarly to distinguish between the subject matter and logical structure of commonsense thinking on the one hand and theoretical thinking on the other and to examine their interrelation (chapter IV). Neither of these investigations will concern itself with the question which of the exhibited logical theories is primary and which secondary. The reason for this neglect is not that the distinction is un-important or uninteresting; but that where it is made, it presents merely another internally incorrigible, but externally corrigible feature of the categorial framework of which it is a characteristic.

In order to show this it will be sufficient to anticipate some of the more general results of the subsequent investigation. As regards the opposition between factual and constructive thinking, it will be argued that the logic appropriate to the former is the 'non-constructive' logic L; and that the logic appropriate to the latter is the 'constructive' logic I. The best-known axiomatization of L is found in *Principia Mathematica*,[1] the best-known axiomatization of I in Heyting's *Intuitionism*.[2] The formal relations between the two systems are well understood: if we add the law of the excluded middle to the constructive system we obtain the non-constructive system.

As regards the opposition between commonsense and theoretical thinking, it will be argued that the logic appropriate to the former admits neutral propositions, while the logic appropriate to the latter does not. For want of better names, I shall call the former logic 'starred', the latter 'unstarred'. The formal relations between the two types of system are again well understood; if we add suitable stipulations about neutral propositions—e.g. to the unstarred classical logic L or to the unstarred constructive logic I—we get a corresponding starred logic $L*$ or $I*$. In our investigation of factual as opposed to constructive and of commonsense as opposed to theoretical thinking, we shall thus be con-cerned with four types of logical theory, namely a starred classical, an unstarred classical, a starred constructive, and an unstarred constructive logic.[3]

Let us now assume that our categorial framework F is rich enough to contain at least four maximal kinds such that each of our four logical theories is appropriate to reasoning about the members of one of these four maximal kinds. Let us further assume that our primary logical theory, i.e. the theory which underlies F, is starred classical. This does not prevent us from legitimately employing the other three logical

---

[1] Vol. 1 (2nd edition, Cambridge, 1925).
[2] Amsterdam, 1956.
[3] See Appendix, p. 79 below.

theories as secondary (auxiliary, fictitious, etc.). Reality, we might for example hold, conforms to starred classical logic. It conforms to starred logic because some of its areas are so hazy or fluid that they are with equal justice described by either members of certain pairs of contradictory propositions (e.g. when a borderline case between 'green' and 'not green' is judged to be one or the other). And it conforms to classical logic because outside its areas of inexactness every proposition about it is either definitely true or definitely false. Yet, we might add, it is a useful fiction for certain purposes (e.g. scientific simplification) to ignore all neutral propositions, i.e. use an unstarred logic; and for certain other purposes (e.g. practical planning) to ignore the law of the excluded middle.

If we hold, or are converted to, the view that, say, unstarred constructive logic is our primary logic, we should argue on the same lines as before. But we should now be committed to the view that reality contains no neutral areas and that it contains, temporarily or permanently, undecided areas which are not subject to the law of excluded middle. At the same time we might regard it as a useful fiction for certain purposes (e.g. commonsense thinking in some everyday transactions) to admit neutral propositions; and for certain other purposes (e.g. the use of classical mathematics in physics) to postulate the law of excluded middle. If the primary logic is starred constructive or unstarred classical, the use of the other three types of logic is again defensible as secondary.

The method of justifying the distinction between primary and secondary logic is analogous to the method of justifying the distinction between independent and dependent particulars. The primary logic, like the autosemantic symbols, is supposed to correspond to reality, whereas a secondary logic, like the synsemantic symbols, lacks such correspondence and refers at best to deliberate fictions. Again, the statements which conform only to a secondary logic can, like synsemantic symbols, be regarded as elliptical, i.e. as in need and capable of being embedded into wider statements which conform to the primary logic. To achieve this it will often suffice to supplement the elliptical statement with the rider 'assuming for the sake of argument the validity of a secondary logic with postulates . . .'.

If the user of a categorial framework F distinguishes explicitly or implicitly the primary logic which underlies F from other logical theories employed by him in thinking about the members of some maximal class of F in a secondary or auxiliary manner, then the rejection of the distinction amounts to a rejection of F, but not thereby also of any F. Indeed among the frameworks replacing F, and differing from it in their primary logic, there will be some which are so similar to F that it is extremely difficult to exhibit the difference. Yet whether the replacement will be very radical or hardly perceptible, its very possibility shows

3

that the distinction between primary and secondary logical systems is internally, but not also externally, incorrigible.

Internal incorrigibility and truth
Just as the internal incorrigibility of a proposition must not be confused with external incorrigibility, so it must also not be confused with truth. The two notions must be different since the incorrigibility of a proposition with regard to a categorial framework consists, by definition, in its being logically implied by the conjunction of propositions describing the framework, whereas the truth of at least some propositions depends on their relation to non-propositional entities. Yet the danger of confusion appears to be serious enough to justify us in elaborating and illustrating the distinction.

For this purpose we assume that a person A employs a categorial framework F with respect to which a proposition g_0 is incorrigible. This does not mean that A has ever considered g_0 nor that he believes g_0 to be incorrigible. He might, for example, not be a good enough reasoner to recognize that the conjunction of propositions describing F logically implies g_0. If, however, A believes g_0 to be internally incorrigible then he will normally also believe that g_0 is not false. (I say 'normally', in order to make allowance for people who claim that they are capable of believing false and even logically impossible propositions, for example, those who claim to say truthfully '*credo quia absurdum*'.) But A may *correctly* believe that g_0 is incorrigible with respect to F—which, among other things, means that g_0 *is* incorrigible with respect to F—when g_0 is false, when g_0 is true, when g_0 is neither verifiable nor falsifiable, or even when g_0 lacks any truth-value.

In order to give an example of a false, and falsified, internally incorrigible proposition we assume that A, by employing F, acknowledges a class of demigods as a maximal kind such that 'being a demigod' logically implies—in accordance with the logic underlying F—the constitutive attribute 'being a descendant of one of the giant immortal gods inhabiting Mount Olympus'. The proposition that at least one of the gods inhabiting Mount Olympus has a descendant, is incorrigible with respect to F and is, or would be, correctly believed by A to be incorrigible. It is nevertheless false and falsified. That A has not falsified g_0 and does not believe that anybody else has done so, might be explained by some features of his religion without committing us to the view that he is less rational that most of us. Examples of internally incorrigible true propositions are readily available. If A, by employing F, acknowledges the class of (non-human) animals as a maximal kind such that 'being an animal' logically implies 'not being a descendant of a giant immortal god inhabiting Mount Olympus', then the proposition that no animal is the descendant of such a god is both incorrigible with respect to F and true. We may even assume that it has been verified by a complete test of the absence of giants on Mount Olympus.

In order to provide an example of an internally incorrigible proposition which is neither verifiable nor falsifiable, we assume that A, by employing F, acknowledges a class of events as a maximal kind with which the principle of causality is associated as one of its constitutive principles. The principle is not verifiable, if only because its verification would mean testing an unlimited number of events; and it is for the same reason not falsifiable. Most, if not all, propositions which are regarded as 'metaphysical' are internally incorrigible, unverifiable and falsifiable propositions.

As for internally incorrigible propositions which, beyond being unverifiable and unfalsifiable, are neither true nor false, it may at first glance seem doubtful whether there are such. If g_0 is to be one of them, it must not only lack truth and falsity, but also be logically implied by a proposition f (characterizing the categorial framework F employed by a person A). Whether or not the two conditions are compatible with each other depends on the logic underlying F. If L underlies F then the two conditions are incompatible: for in (the standard interpretation of) L nothing but a proposition logically implies or is logically implied; and nothing is a proposition unless it is true or false. If, however, I underlies F then, since I admits propositions which are neither true nor false (in the standard interpretation of I), a proposition which is neither true nor false may be incorrigible with respect to F and—moreover—A may believe it to be true.

It is worth noting that L can be so extended that logical implications become permissible between 'propositions' in a wider sense, covering also truth-value-free entities such as rules, proposals, decisions, resolutions. However, even if L is thus enlarged, we should have to explain first, how truth-value-less propositions of the enlarged logic can stand in logical relations not only to each other but also to propositions with truth-value; and second, in what sense, some rules, proposals, decisions, resolutions, etc. can be 'believed'. To do so, even if it were possible, would here be a superfluous task. For although some of the subsequent arguments will presuppose the possibility of internally incorrigible propositions which are unverifiable and unfalsifiable, none will depend on the assumption of internally incorrigible propositions which are neither true nor false.

UNIVERSITY OF BRISTOL
Department of Philosophy

9 Woodland Road
Bristol
BS8 1TB

Chapter III

Constructive thinking about alternative expectable, practicable, or optional developments, and non-constructive thinking about unalterable facts or developments are, at least *prima facie*, interdependent. The exploration of alternative possibilities seems to require the recognition of an unalterable common background for their realization, while the search for what is unalterable seems to presuppose attempts at supplanting it by actual or imagined alternatives. Thinking in most fields appears to possess both a constructive and a non-constructive aspect, even though the emphasis on one at the expense of the other and their mutual adjustment may greatly differ from field to field and thinker to thinker.

The purpose of this chapter is to show how the contrast between constructive and non-constructive thinking affects the general structure of categorial frameworks in a characteristic manner. It is, more particularly, to exhibit the assumptions—be they ontological or merely heuristic—by which constructive thinking differs from non-constructive; to compare the logical structure of constructive and non-constructive thinking; to indicate some general differences in the constitution of the maximal kinds employed in constructive as opposed to non-constructive thinking; and lastly to consider various possibilities of their mutual adjustment in the light of our earlier distinction between primary and secondary logical theories and between independent and dependent particulars.

On the assumptions of branching and branchless sequences of situations

By 'a situation' I shall understand a conjunction of characteristics which may characterize a region of space during an interval of time. The term covers not only situations in the narrow sense which implies a temporary absence of change, but also processes and events of short or long duration. Situations of one kind or another might be conceived as independent particulars on the existence of which, for example, the existence of physical objects depends; or, conversely, as dependent particulars the existence of which depends on the existence of physical objects. We may safely say that the subject matter, as we know it, of both factual and constructive thinking includes particulars which either are situations or are located in situations, and that it also includes sequences of situations. Before comparing and contrasting the logical and categorial structure of factual and constructive thinking, it is necessary to distinguish between various assumptions about the manner in which different sequences of situations may be related to each other.

In representing sequences of situations I shall largely follow A. Grzegorczyk.[1] A sequence of situations will be represented as a sequence of points on a directed line. Each situation is characterized by an 'information set', i.e. a set of atomic propositions—an atomic proposition being one the assertion of which is the application of a one-, two-, ..., n-place attribute to one, two, ..., n-individuals in a certain order, e.g. 'John is a man'; 'John is taller than Charles' ('Charles is taller than John'); etc. The individuals may be dependent or independent so long as they are present in the characterized situation. I shall use small Greek letters with or without subscripts, e.g. α, β_1, β_2, ..., for information sets and small Roman letters p to w, with or without subscripts, e.g. p, q_1, q_2, ..., for atomic propositions which are the members of information sets. In order to distinguish variables from constants the latter will be written with subscripts.

The development of a sequence of situations corresponds to an increase of information about it. Assume that the first situation is characterized by the consistent information set $\alpha_0 = \{p_1 \ldots p_n\}$ and that the second situation involves an increase of information about the sequence over and above α_0 by, say, $\{q_1 \ldots q_k\}$. This will be expressed by associating $\beta_0 = \{p_1 \ldots p_n; q_1 \ldots q_k\}$ with the second situation so that β_0 includes and extends the information contained in α_0. We proceed in the same manner for the third and every subsequent situation so that every information set includes and extends its predecessors. Writing '$\alpha \prec \beta$' for 'β is an extension of α', we can characterize the different stages discerned in an actual or imagined walk, war, plan, etc. by, say, $\alpha \prec \beta \prec \gamma \prec \delta \prec \cdots$. Clearly, if $\alpha \prec \beta$ and $\beta \prec \gamma$ then $\alpha \prec \gamma$.

An initial or intermediate situation in a sequence of situations may be 'nodal' in the sense that it is an initial situation of at least two different sequences of situations. Each of these sequences may in turn contain nodal situations. Let us call a system of such branching sequences a 'perfect tree' if, and only if, it contains an initial situation and if every

[1] A. Grzegorczyk, *A philosophically plausible formal interpretation of intuitionist logic*, Indagationes Mathematicae, vol. 26 (1964), pp. 596–601. (Grzegorczyk uses the term 'information set' for the class of all sets which in this chapter are called 'information sets'.) For another interpretation (in terms of pseudo-Boolean algebras) see H. Rasiowa and R. Sikorski, *The Mathematics of Metamathematics* (2nd revised edition, Warsaw, 1968).

situation which is not final is nodal. The following diagram represents
a perfect tree of situations:

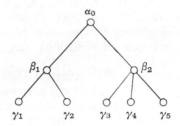

An 'imperfect tree' contains apart from final situations and from nodal
situations, which lie on the intersections of at least two branches, also
'intervening' situations, which (like the situations marked by the crosses
in the diagram on p. 35) lie between, but not on, such intersections.[1]

   The purely formal distinction between trees and branchless sequences
of situations does not imply any thesis concerning their real existence.
Indeed, if one is to give a tolerably clear formulation of various ontological assumptions of branching and branchlessness, one has to endow
some of our information sets and their extensions with empirically un-
discoverable characteristics. Let us say that an information set is 'fully
characteristic' of a situation or sequence of situations if and only if, it
contains an answer to every question about the situation or the sequence
except to the questions about its spatio-temporal location or about its
extensions. Let us say that an information set β is an 'ontologically
admissible' extension of an information set α if and only if α and β are
fully characteristic and $\alpha \prec \beta$ is not excluded by some permanent
feature of the universe such as the laws of nature, divine providence,
etc. Lastly, let us say that an information set is 'critical' if and only if it
is fully characteristic of a situation or sequence of situations which has
actually occurred, while (as yet) none of its ontologically admissible
extensions have occurred. A critical information set thus separates what
has happened from what might happen afterwards.

   We now formulate some ontological assumptions in terms of 'critical
information set' and 'ontologically admissible extension': (i) The
assumption of branchlessness or predetermination: For every critical
information set α there exists one and only one extension β which is
ontologically admissible (strictly speaking one and only one expanding
sequence of extensions, e.g. $\alpha \prec \beta \prec \gamma \prec \cdots$). (ii) The assumption of

---

[1] Formally the relation $\prec$ which orders the elements of a (perfect or imperfect)
tree is characterized as follows: It is (I) reflexive, (II) antisymmetrical, and
(III) transitive. Moreover, (IV) if $\alpha \prec \gamma$ and $\beta \prec \gamma$, then either $\alpha \prec \beta$ or $\beta \prec \alpha$;
and (V) there is an origin α_0 such that for all β—not ($\beta \prec \alpha_0$).

branching: For every critical information set there exist at least two ontologically admissible extensions. As regards the number of these extensions one might distinguish (a) unrestricted branching: every extension of α is ontologically admissible; (b) restricted, infinite branching: an infinite subclass of the class of extensions of α is ontologically admissible; (c) restricted finite branching: a finite subclass of the class of extensions of α is ontologically admissible.

Further possibilities might be considered. Among them is a possible reduction of the number of branches in the course of time. Thus one of an infinite number of admissible extensions may lead through a nodal information set with a finite number of admissible extensions which might in due course become a critical information set. Again, one might have to consider whether different ontologically admissible extensions are significantly different. It may for example be the case that the infinitely numerous admissible extensions according to (iib) are so similar to each other that in practice (iib) and (i) are indistinguishable.

By according the status of an ontological truth to one of the mentioned assumptions one is not precluded from using the others in an auxiliary manner. A person who adopts an ontological assumption of branching may still employ classical physics—even if he holds that classical physics implies branchlessness. A person who adopts the ontological assumption of branchlessness may still employ the frequency-theory of probability—even if he holds that this theory implies branching. Consistency can always be achieved by demoting the rejecting ontological assumption to a mere heuristic or auxiliary principle. Indeed for many purposes it is not necessary to decide which of the incompatible assumptions is ontological and which merely auxiliary.

On the logical structure of constructive and factual thinking

The term 'constructive thinking' will henceforth be used in the sense of thinking about (or rather representable by) trees of situations—a type of thinking whose underlying logic will turn out to be *I*. The terms 'non-constructive thinking' or 'factual thinking' will be used in the sense of any kind of thinking whose underlying logic is *L*. Concentrating on these special paradigms will not, I believe, result in any real loss of philosophical generality, and has the great advantage of enabling one to make use of recent work in logic which has led to a deeper understanding of these important paradigmatic cases.[1]

Consider a tree T_0. If for each point of T_0 we know its associated information set, we possess the maximal amount of information about T_0. We may, however, also be interested in information of a more special

---

[1] Although the proposed technical uses of 'constructive' and 'non-constructive' ('factual') diverge from the ordinary uses of these words, I could not think of a more convenient terminology.

kind, e.g. in questions concerning the manner in which some of the available information is distributed over T_0. Such questions can be asked and answered in terms of a characteristic relation between information sets, trees and propositions. It is expressed by saying that an information set, say α_0, secures a proposition, say g_0, on a tree T_0, and by writing $\alpha_0 \Vdash_{T_0} g_0$. The secured proposition may be either atomic or formed from atomic propositions by means of the connectives AND, OR, NOT, IF–THEN, or the quantifiers THERE EXISTS and FOR ALL. The capitalized expressions do not necessarily have the same meaning as the similar-sounding words 'and', 'or', etc. of ordinary English, whose meaning will for the present be taken as understood.

With this *proviso*—using 'g' and 'h' as variables ranging over propositions '$P(x)$' as a predicate-variable, 'α' as a variable ranging over information sets and 'T' as a variable ranging over trees—we define $\alpha \Vdash_T g$ (an information set α secures a proposition g on a tree T) as follows: (i) If g is atomic then $\alpha \Vdash_T g$ if, and only if, however we proceed from α (on T towards more inclusive information sets) we reach an extension β of α ($\alpha \prec \beta$) such that g is an element of β. (ii) $\alpha \Vdash_T g$ AND h if, and only if, $\alpha \Vdash_T g$ and $\alpha \Vdash_T h$. (iii) $\alpha \Vdash_T g$ OR h if, and only if, however we proceed from α we reach an extension β of α such that $\beta \Vdash_T g$ or $\beta \Vdash_T h$. (iv) $\alpha \Vdash_T$ NOT-g, if, and only if, however we proceed from α we do not reach an extension β of α such that $\beta \Vdash_T g$. (v) $\alpha \Vdash_T$ IF g THEN h if, and only if, either not $\alpha \Vdash_T g$ or $\alpha \Vdash_T h$ or both. (vi) $\alpha \Vdash_T$ THERE EXISTS an x such that $P(x)$ if, and only if, however we proceed from α, we reach an extension β of α such that $\beta \Vdash_T P(a)$ for some individual a. (vii) $\alpha \Vdash_T$ FOR ALL x $P(x)$ if, and only if, $\alpha \Vdash_T P(a)$ for every individual a.

Different information sets on the same tree, as well as the same information set on different trees will in general secure different propositions. This does not exclude the interesting possibility of propositions which are secured by *every* information set on *every* tree. If there are such propositions and if they can be systematically exhibited or generated, then their system would characterize the general structure of constructive thinking, conceived as thinking about trees of situations, to such an extent as to deserve the name of a formal theory of constructive thinking or even of constructive logic.

Using results of Tarski and Beth, Grzegorczyk (op. cit.) has proved that the class of propositions which are secured by every information set on every tree coincides with the class of valid principles of intuitionist logic. The proof, which will not be reproduced here, is philosophically significant in at least three respects. First of all, it enables one to give a clear sense to the thesis that intuitionist logic is the logic of constructive mathematics. Second, it shows that in this sense intuitionist logic may quite generally be regarded as the logic of constructive thinking of which constructive mathematics is only a species. Third, it makes possible a better understanding of the relation between constructive and factual thinking. We shall here be concerned only with some aspects of the second and third points.[1]

Let us indicate that a propositional form g is a principle of constructive logic, i.e. that it is secured by every information set on every tree by writing $\Vdash g$, since it is in this case not necessary to mention a specific information set or a specific tree. For example, we have $\Vdash$ IF g THEN NOT-NOT g and $\Vdash$ NOT (g AND NOT g). The most striking feature of constructive logic is, as has been mentioned already, the absence from it of the law of excluded middle and the consequent absence of some other principles. Obvious examples showing the invalidity of the principle of excluded middle in constructive logic can now be easily given. Assuming that on the tree T_0 of the above diagram the atomic proposition p_0 is contained in β_1 and consequently in γ_1 and γ_2, but that it is not contained in any other information set, we have: $not\ \alpha \Vdash_T p_0$ (by (i)), $not\ \alpha \Vdash_T$ NOT p_0 (by (iv)) and $not\ \alpha \Vdash_T p_0$ OR NOT p_0 (by (iii)). The last expression is the desired counterexample since it exemplifies an information set, a tree, and a proposition such that the set does not secure the disjunction of the proposition and its (constructive) negation on the tree.

In defining the manner in which information sets on trees secure atomic and non-atomic propositions I have emphasized the difference between the capitalized logical particles 'AND', 'OR', 'NOT', ..., which occur in the defined expressions and the normally printed logical particles 'and', 'or', 'not', ..., which occur in the defining expressions. The latter were treated as well-understood words of ordinary English which can be left undefined. Even if this procedure is defensible, it is possible to define these particles more precisely as the particles of the logic (or a fragment of the logic) of factual thinking, namely L. The logical principles of constructive logic are than [then] qua 'propositions secured by every information set on every tree' defined in terms of the logical principles of classical logic.

Grzegorczyk's interpretation of constructive logic in terms of factual logic clearly shows that, and how, a thinker who employs both systems in his thinking may regard classical logic as primary and constructive logic as secondary. But it is equally possible to regard constructive logic as primary—e.g. because all thinking is 'ultimately' constructive—and to interpret the factual logic in terms of it.[2] The reasons why the former

[1] For thorough discussions from the point of view of formal logic and for guides to the literature see S. Kripke's 'Semantical analysis of intuitionist logic' in *Formal Systems and Recursive Functions* (ed. by Crossley and Dummett, Amsterdam, 1965); K. Schütte, *Vollständige Systeme Modaler und Intuitionistischer Logik* (Berlin, 1968); A. Mostowski, *Thirty Years of Foundational Studies* (Oxford, 1966).

[2] For an interpretation of classical in terms of intuitionist logic, see K. Gödel, *Zum intuitionistischen Aussagenkalkül* Ergebnisse eines mathematischen Kolloquiums, Heft 4 (1933), p. 40.

procedure may seem preferable are historical rather than philosophical. Most mathematical theories employed by scientists are embedded in classical elementary logic which has, consequently, attracted the main attention from logicians and philosophers. Only lately have the claims for absolute primacy of factual logic begun to be counterbalanced by claims for the absolute primacy of constructive logic. From the point of view of this essay the primacy of either logic is, as has been argued already, an internally incorrigible but externally corrigible feature of the categorial framework to which it belongs. And it must be emphasized that by calling elementary classical logic 'factual' and elementary intuitionist logic 'constructive' I am *not* implying that these systems cannot be varied or extended. Indeed the next chapter will introduce a variant for each of the two systems of factual and constructive logic.

In order to avoid an unnecessary proliferation of symbols by using different signs for the logical particles and expressions of L and I, I shall prefix propositions containing particles of L by 'L:' and propositions containing particles of I by 'I:'. In a similar way logically valid propositional forms and propositions of L will sometimes be prefixed by '$\vdash_L$', valid propositional forms and propositions of I by '$\vdash_I$'. Thus $\vdash_L p \vee \neg p$, $\vdash_L \neg\neg p \rightarrow p$, $\vdash_L (\neg p \rightarrow \neg q) \rightarrow (q \rightarrow p)$; whereas in I: $(p \vee \neg p)$, $I: (\neg\neg p \rightarrow p)$, $I: (\neg p \rightarrow \neg q) \rightarrow (q \rightarrow p)$ the '$(I:)$' is not replaceable by '$\vdash_I$'. A more detailed comparison between I and L is not necessary for our present purpose.[1]

On the categorial structure of factual and constructive thinking

In turning our attention to the categorial structure of factual and constructive thinking, it will be convenient to consider categorial frameworks which are embedded in L and in which I, in accordance with the above interpretation in terms of L, functions as a secondary logic. In accepting this restriction one should remember that categorial frameworks in which this rôle of L and I is reversed are perfectly feasible. For the moment, however, we are not interested in the ontological priority of L over I or I over L, but in the categorial content which can be accommodated by them.

About the application and applicability of L to reasoning about many kinds of objects little needs to be said. There is no scarcity of more or less carefully analysed examples of categorial frameworks or parts of them which are embedded in L. Indeed until the advent of intuitionism no other logical system was admitted in either a primary or a secondary rôle. Categorial frameworks proposed or examined by philosophers from Aristotle to Kant and beyond were assumed to presuppose L in the sense that every logical term employed in a categorization or formulation of a constitutive or individuating principle was without

[1] For such a comparison see the Appendix.

question regarded as belonging to L. The same is true of most categorial frameworks employed by scientists. What needs to be discussed, therefore, is not so much the natural applicability and application of L as these of I—in particular outside the domain of mathematics.

I, as we have seen, is the logic of constructive thinking in the precise sense in which such thinking is (representable as thinking) about trees of situations. The categorial, as opposed to the merely logical, structure of constructive thinking depends not merely on its being about trees in general but on its being about specified kinds of trees. Among them the trees employed in practical thinking are of particular interest, since every practical thinker, whatever his ontological convictions, regards himself as placed in sequences of situations which contain nodal situations with branches the realization of which depends on the exercise of options. It may be, and has been, argued that in the ultimate analysis all actual thinking is constructive and more particularly practical. But, whatever the merits of such arguments, practical thinking is an important species of constructive thinking. We may best conceive practical thinking as thinking governed by the logical theory I in conjunction with some further non-logical principles or constraints on the construction of trees.

Even if practical thinking can be characterized as thinking about the exercise of options and, therefore, as representable by trees consisting of optional sequences of situations, the concepts employed in it may greatly differ from one categorial framework to another. Thus a maximal kind might consist of persons defined as beings which not only exercise options, but also are endowed with an immortal soul or lacking it; of materials defined not only as capable of being acted upon by persons in the exercise of options, but also as bits of matter subject to laws of nature of widely different sorts; of actions defined not only as beings, or being connected with, optional conduct, but also as subject to moral evaluation in accordance with a variety of different moral systems. In attending to the common categorial structure of practical thinking one is not denying these or other differences.

If a sequence of situations is optional, then it is also practicable; and if it is practicable then it is also empirically possible. But an empirically possible sequence of situations need not be practicable, and a practicable sequence of situations need not be optional. In order to make these notions more precise, we assume that a person believes or imagines himself to be in a situation which he describes by an information set α_0 and that the developments which he regards as empirically possible are represented by our tree diagram. He thus considers empirically possible the developments $\alpha_0 \prec \beta_1 \prec \gamma_1, \alpha_0 \prec \beta_1 \prec \gamma_2, \alpha_0 \prec \beta_2 \prec \gamma_3, \alpha_0 \prec \beta_2 \prec \gamma_4$, and $\alpha_0 \prec \beta_2 \prec \gamma_5$. He might, of course, have constructed an altogether different 'expectability-tree' as I shall call any tree representing alternative developments assumed to be empirically possible by its constructor. Yet any expectability-tree would have to satisfy not only I but in addition also the requirement that every development be compatible with the factual beliefs of the tree's designer. For example $\alpha_0 \prec \beta_1 \prec \gamma_1$ must not be the description of a river flowing uphill. The restrictive condition of the compatibility of a tree-construction with its designer's empirical beliefs demarcates the domain of constructive thinking about empirically possible developments. Constructive thinking of this kind is implied in practical thinking —even though by itself it need not be concerned with either options or practicabilities.

The construction of expectability-trees in contexts demanding a decision between real or apparent alternatives is justifiable both by a metaphysical indeterminist and a metaphysical determinist. The former will justify his procedure both by his lack of empirical knowledge and his assumption that nature is a branching system, the latter only by his lack of empirical knowledge. The actual construction of an expectability-tree will depend not only on its designer's empirical beliefs but also on his imagination. Of two medical, economic, or other experts sharing the same empirical beliefs the more imaginative will construct richer expectability-trees.

Some empirically possible developments are also practicable. Let us, in accordance with the interpretation of our diagram as an expectability-tree, call the information sets $\alpha_0, \beta_1, \beta_2, \gamma_1, \gamma_2, \gamma_3, \gamma_4, \gamma_5$ 'expectation sets'. Let us assume that the designer of the tree believes that finding himself in the situation (described by) α_0 he 'can bring about' either β_1 or β_2 by suitably chosen bodily conduct. Such conduct is describable by an ordered set of atomic propositions, e.g. a set of propositions describing the stages in a person's loading a gun and pressing its trigger. I shall call these sets which describe chosen bodily conduct as 'conduct sets'. Let ξ_1 and ξ_2 be two mutually incompatible conduct sets such that neither ξ_1 or ξ_2 are included in α_0 and such that ξ_1 is included in β_1 and ξ_2 is included in β_2. In other words, between the nodal sets α_0 and β_1 there lies a non-nodal set $\alpha_0 \cup \xi_1$, and between the nodal sets α_0 and β_2 there lies a non-nodal set $\alpha_0 \cup \xi_2$. These intervening sets (each of which is the union of α_0 and a conduct set) might be called 'intervention sets' because they intervene between two expectation sets and because they describe interventions in the course of events of which the designer of the tree thinks himself capable. The diagram on page 35 represents these relations.

The domains of constructive thinking about practical and optional developments can now be demarcated in terms of further conditions imposed on expectability-trees by their designers. An expectability-tree is a practicability-tree if, and only if, its designer believes that it contains

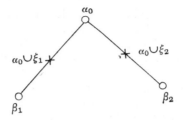

an intervention set between any two successive expectation sets. A practicability-tree is an option-tree if, and only if, its designer *believes* that his choice to realize an intervention set and his realization of it is 'free' in the sense of not being wholly predetermined by situations preceding his chosen conduct. The questions whether his belief is every true and, if so, how it can be reconciled with the best available empirical knowledge must be separated from the empirical fact that the belief is being held.[1]

A more detailed examination of the categorial structure of practical thinking would have to proceed along at least two lines. First, it would have to consider moral and prudential evaluations as imposing further conditions on the construction of option-trees. Second, it would have to venture beyond emphasizing a general connection between the constitution of maximal kinds, employed in practical thinking, and substantive extensions of the logical theory *I*, by exhibiting in detail the categorial structure of practical thinking in different, specific frameworks or types of them. Instead of pursuing these tasks, which fall outside the scope of this essay, I shall—again in a general way—consider the interaction of factual and constructive thinking when both are united in the same categorial framework, employed by the same person.

On the mutual adjustment of constructive and factual thinking

Although of the two logical theories *L* and *I* only one can underly a categorial framework as its primary logic, the other can nevertheless be employed as a secondary logical theory. The ontological priority of one logic over the other is at most only internally incorrigible, and either logic can be interpreted in terms of the other. In passing from the logical to the substantive (non-logical) propositions of factual and constructive thinking, one is once again faced with apparently conflicting claims to ontological priority. Thus statements about what is, has been or will be the case or about what is the case at all times or extratemporally seem to be clearly factual, whereas statements about as yet unexercised options seem clearly constructive. Which, if any, of the two

[1] For a discussion of these questions, see *What is Philosophy?—One Philosopher's Answer*, ch. XIV.

kinds of proposition should be regarded as primary and which as secondary, i.e. interpretable in terms of the other? Either decision is feasible and capable of fairly simple implementation.

In order to show this, it will be convenient to consider the difference between factual and constructive beliefs in the light of the Beth-Grzegorczyk model of constructive thinking. In stating one's belief in a factual truth, e.g. that Brutus murdered Caesar or that magnetized pieces of iron attract iron filings, one is (at least *prima facie*) not referring to any tree-construction. In stating one's belief in a constructive truth, e.g. that one has the options of taking the high road or the low road, one is (at least *prima facie*) referring to tree-constructions. A person holding this belief might, for example, express it by saying that he would find it 'natural' to construct an option-tree which would contain these options or that he would find it natural so to extend any of his already constructed option-trees as to make it contain this option. These suggestions can be expressed more generally and more precisely.

Consider a constructive domain, say of expectability-, practicability-, or option-trees, and let g_0 be a statement which, though well-formed in accordance with I, is not logically necessary or valid in I, I shall say that g_0 expresses a person's constructive conjecture about a feature of D if, and only if, g_0 is secured on one of the trees which the person has constructed in D. I shall say that g_0 expresses a person's constructive conjecture about a *regularity* of D if, and only if, the person can (consistently with his relevant beliefs) so continue the construction of every already constructed tree that g_0 is secured on the augmented tree (i.e. the tree resulting from continuing the construction of the already constructed tree). Let us illustrate the two kinds of conjecture in the constructive domain of option-trees: My conjecture that I have the option of taking the high road to Scotland is a constructive conjecture of a feature of D since I have constructed an option-tree on which the option is secured. But it is not a constructive conjecture of a regularity of D since (we assume) on one of my already constructed option-trees I have secured the option of suicide in conditions the realization of which may precede any of my options to leave Bristol. On the other hand the implication that *if* I shall travel to Scotland, I shall do so on the high road expresses my constructive conjecture of a regularity since I can (we assume) so continue every one of my already constructed option-trees as to secure this implication on it.

Compared with the notion of constructive conjectures the notion of factual or non-constructive conjectures is so familiar that it need not be expressed in detail. They are made about features or regularities of a factual, i.e. pre-existing or predetermined region of the world. While, roughly speaking, factual conjectures are about facts and constructive conjectures about constructibilities, it is feasible to conceive of constructibilities as a species of facts, to conceive of facts as a species of constructibilities and so oscillate systematically between the two conceptions.

Let us start with the reinterpretation of constructive as factual conjectures. A constructive conjecture about a feature or regularity in a constructive domain can always be regarded as merely auxiliary and as replaceable without loss by a factual conjecture about an occurrent or dispositional property of the pre-existing or predetermined world. Thus, if 'All magnetized pieces of iron attract iron filings' expresses a constructive conjecture about regularities in the constructive domain of expectable, practicable, or optional developments, it may be reinterpreted as a factual conjecture about pre-existing particulars with certain dispositional properties, e g. the property of magnetizability. The transition from a constructive conjecture ($I: g_0$) to a factual conjecture ($L: g_0$) may be implemented technically by regarding the former statement as an elliptical version of the latter. The absorption of constructive conjectures and constructive truths by factual conjectures and factual truths is characteristic of many versions of so-called realist, naturalist, or materialist metaphysics.

The reinterpretation of factual as constructive conjectures is the mirror image of the reinterpretation just discussed. Thus, if 'All magnetized pieces of iron attract iron filings' expresses a factual conjecture, it may be reinterpreted as a constructive conjecture about regularities in the constructive domain of expectable, practicable, or optional developments. This absorption of factual conjectures and truths by constructive ones is characteristic of some versions of modern operationalism and verificationism and some older so-called idealist systems of metaphysics.

There is no absolute need for the total assimilation of constructibilities to facts or facts to constructibilities. Indeed most people in their ordinary concerns seem to be unwilling to expose themselves to the intellectual strains resulting from either kind of totalitarianism. One conception of constructive and factual thinking as interdependent and interlocking can be indicated by the following picture of a cyclic process: (i) Constructions in a constructive domain D subject to the requirement of their compatibility with the factual beliefs demarcating D. (Thus the construction of expectability-trees must not violate our commonsense or physical beliefs about the physical universe.) (ii) Making constructive conjectures about regularities in D. (iii) Exposing the constructive conjectures to appropriate tests (which in the case of conjectures about regular expectabilities include physical experiments). (iv) Reinterpretation of constructive conjectures which stood up well to the relevant tests as factual beliefs. (v) Incorporation of these factual beliefs among those demarcating D. (vi) = (i) except for the additional factual beliefs.

Since the picture of the 'fact-construction-cycle' is highly schematic some remarks guarding it against misunderstanding seem to be in place. First, it must not be assumed that the very first starting point of a person's thinking consists in making factual assumptions or in constructing trees. At the stage of development at which factual and constructive thinking are reflectively distinguishable the question of temporal priority is as pointless as the question about which came first—the hen or the egg. Second, it must also not be assumed that the factual beliefs which demarcate a constructive domain are continually increased without radical revisions. Lastly, it must not be overlooked that in filling in the details of the schematic picture the differences between the various constructive domains have to be considered as carefully as their similarities. Such considerations, however, would transcend the scope of this essay.

Since a person's categorial framework, say F, is employed by him both in his constructive and factual thinking we may distinguish between the constructive and factual maximal kinds of F. A constructive maximal kind consists of constructible or constructed, a factual maximal kind of pre-existent objects. If the user of F assumes the primacy of factual over constructive logic then his constructive maximal kinds will be dependent, and at least one of his factual maximal kinds independent. If he assumes the primacy of constructive over factual logic then his factual maximal kinds will be dependent, and at least one of his constructive maximal kinds independent. He may, however, make no assumption about the primacy of either logic—thus leaving the problem of the independence of constructible or pre-existent objects open, or deciding it on other grounds.

Chapter IV

The purpose of this chapter is to examine the logical and categorial structure of categorial frameworks in so far as their employment involves a more or less radical distinction between commonsense concepts and assumptions on the one hand, and theoretical or scientific ones on the other. The distinction covers both factual and constructive thinking. Its basis is not that the aims of science—prediction, explanation, and mastery of natural phenomena—are foreign to commonsense, but rather that science pursues them in a more methodical manner. Scientific investigation is more specialized, its intellectual outcome more tightly organized and its testable content exposed to more stringent public tests. The division of science into the various special sciences makes for a high degree of conceptual and categorial economy. The tight organization of scientific theories makes for a high degree of logical exactness and unification. While we shall pay attention to both these aspects, the nature and importance of public testability and expert consensus in science will not concern us here.

In contrasting commonsense and theoretical thinking and in exhibiting their interconnection, it will be convenient to proceed as follows. After making a fairly obvious distinction between axiomatic and other scientific theories, commonsense and theoretical thinking will be compared, first in respect of their logical, and secondly in respect of their categorial structure. On the basis of these comparisons it will be shown how the logic and the maximal kinds of commonsense on the one hand and of theorizing on the other are jointly employed in the application of theory to experience. The chapter will be concluded with some brief remarks on the problem of ontological primacy as it arises for the logic and objects of commonsense on the one hand and of scientific theorizing on the other.

Axiomatic and other scientific theories

The most characteristic outcome of scientific thinking are scientific theories. Among them those which have been formulated as axiomatic systems are for the moment particularly instructive. A theory is formulated as an axiomatic system in the strongest sense of the term if all its

4

non-logical and logical assumptions and rules of inference have been explicitly stated; in a weaker sense if all its non-logical assumptions have been explicitly stated; and in the weakest sense if those non-logical assumptions have been explicitly stated which the consensus of experts does not regard as too obvious to be worth explicit mention. Scientists have on the whole aimed at presenting their theories as axiomatic systems in the weaker or weakest sense of the term and have tended to regard the more usual presentations of Newtonian dynamics as good examples of an axiomatically formulated scientific theory.

It is customary to distinguish between the substantive content of an axiomatic system and its formal structure. The distinction is by no means absolute. Whereas the elementary logic underlying the system (i.e. propositional logic, quantification theory, and theory of identity) is usually regarded as part of the system's formal structure, its mathematical concepts and axioms, if any, are sometimes regarded as formal, sometimes as substantive. In accordance with the practice of the preceding chapters only the underlying logic of an axiomatic system will be considered as formal. We shall, therefore, regard all the remaining concepts and propositions as substantive, and shall, as before, attend only to those which form part of the system's categorial structure, that is to say its mathematical and non-mathematical maximal kinds and their associated constitutive and individuating principles.

Let us consider classical dynamics as an illustration. Its underlying logic is L.[1] The maximal kinds acknowledged by the theory are the class of physical particles and, at least in some of its versions, two classes consisting each of only one particular namely space and time. The constitutive attributes of a physical particle are the attributes of possessing a certain mass, of occupying at any moment of time a certain region of space, and of being subject to 'causal laws' (which are conceived by Kant and others as laws expressible in differentiable functions). The constitutive attributes of space and time are their divisibility into elements (especially intervals of a certain length or duration), the interrelations of which are respectively described by Euclidean geometry and chronometry. The individuating attribute of a physical particle is its spatial distance from the origin of a fixed co-ordinate system and its temporal distance from a fixed moment of time. The individuating attributes of space and time are their being the only particulars of their respective kinds.

The constitutive and individuating attributes of the physical particles are quantitative attributes. That is to say, the masses, lengths, durations,

---

[1] This is particularly obvious if we consider presentations of the theory as axiomatic systems in the strongest sense. For relevant papers and bibliography see, e.g., *The Axiomatic Method—With Special Reference to Geometry and Physics*, edited by L. Henkin, P. Suppes, and A. Tarski (Amsterdam, 1959).

distances, etc. in terms of which the motions of particles are (according to the laws of motion) described and predicted are quantities. Quantities, although they are *not* numbers (but ordered pairs whose first members are non-numerical objects and whose second members are numbers), can be subjected to addition, multiplication by a number, and to other theoretical operations which, although they are *not* mathematical, are yet isomorphic with mathematical operations on (natural, rational, and real) numbers. Quantities, moreover, may stand in functional relations which, although not mathematical, are isomorphic with such relations.[1]

Classical dynamics is only one of many instances of an axiomatically presented theory the logical structure of which is non-constructive or factual in the sense of being embedded in L. It is equally only one of many instances of an axiomatically presented theory whose categorial structure, in so far as it is quantitative, is subject to the requirement that the relations between quantities be expressed in terms of classical mathematics, whose underlying logic is again L. But, as we have seen, intuitionist mathematics is embedded in I and there is no reason why intuitionist mathematics should not be employed as the logic underlying such practical theories as welfare economics or decision theory or indeed even the physical sciences conceived in Bridgmanian fashion as operational or as otherwise constructive.[2] Nor can all attempts at embedding scientific theories in many-valued logics be rejected as *a priori* doomed to failure. Since, however, apart from some very few recent exceptions all axiomatic scientific theories are embedded in L, I shall, in comparing theoretical with commonsense thinking, mainly refer to such theories. This restriction is not serious so long as the logical features of theoretical thinking which will be illustrated by reference to L are also characteristic of I (and other 'unstarred' logics mentioned in the Appendix).

The difference between axiomatic and non-axiomatic theories lies neither in their underlying logic nor in their categorial structure, but in their different arrangement of premisses and conclusions. In an axiomatic theory every premiss is either an axiom or a theorem, i.e. directly or indirectly deduced from one or more axioms. In a non-axiomatic theory there are no axioms or theorems. But this does not mean that in such a theory the transition from premisses to conclusions may not proceed in accordance with the same logical principles that govern the inferences within an axiomatic theory. The logic underlying a non-axiomatic scientific theory may thus be again L—as is indeed usually the case.

---

[1] See *Experience and Theory*, ch. X.
[2] See P. Bridgman, *The Nature of Physical Theory* (New York, 1928).

On the logical structure of theoretical as compared with commonsense thinking

The logical structure of scientific theories is best brought out by considering the two types of deduction by which the content of a scientific theory is made explicit. They are (i) the deduction of substantive, i.e. non-logical and non-mathematical, theorems from the axioms of the theory, e.g. the deduction of the law of free fall from the laws of motion; and (ii) the deduction of an unknown state-description from a given state-description in conjunction with the substantive axioms of the theory, e.g. when a statement describing the unknown position of a freely falling body at a certain time is deduced from its position at an earlier time in conjunction with the law of free fall and thus ultimately the laws of motion. The first type of deduction is, as in our example, usually presupposed in deductions of the second type and raises no particular problems. The second type of deduction is best examined in its customary schematic representation as:

$$(s_1 \text{ and } A) \vdash_L s_2$$

In words, from the given state-description s_1 and the non-logical axioms A of the theory the state-description s_2 is deducible in accordance with the principles of the logic L.

The state-descriptions and the axioms are formulated on the one hand in the specific vocabulary of the scientific theory, e.g. in terms of quantities of mass, distance, and duration; on the other hand in the vocabulary of the mathematical theory used in expressing functional relations between these quantities, e.g. the differential and integral calculus. The logical theory by means of which the deducibility $(\cdots \vdash_L \cdots)$ of s_2 from the conjunction of s_1 and A is established, imposes certain requirements upon the premises and the conclusion of the deduction which are *not* in general satisfied by the propositions of commonsense and the vocabulary in which they are expressed. These requirements are (i) that every attribute be extensionally definite or exact; (ii) that the truth-value of every proposition be definite, i.e. truth or falsehood; (iii) that every equality or indistinguishability-relation be reflexive, symmetric, and transitive.

By the extensional definiteness or exactness of an attribute we understand that the class of objects possessing the attribute does not admit of neutral or borderline cases, i.e. objects which can with equal correctness be assigned or refused membership of the class. In L this possibility is simply excluded by the law of excluded middle according to which, given any particular and any class—the particular either is a member or a non-member of the class. But, as is worth emphasizing, the invalidity of the principle of excluded middle in a logical theory does not amount to admission of borderline cases. Thus in I, where the principle is invalid, neutral cases are not admitted (while a logical theory is conceivable which acknowledges more than two truth-values and at the same time borderline cases 'between' them).

Commonsense thinking and the logic underlying it do not satisfy the requirement of the exactness of all attributes. Many, possibly all, of its classifications rely on the recognition of similarities of objects to standard examples and to standard counterexamples. As a result of this the classes corresponding to perceptual and other commonsense-attributes, e.g. 'green' or 'kind', lack the definite extension assumed by L and required by any scientific theory embedded in L.[1] However adequately an inexact attribute may represent the features of our experience with its occasional fluidity and lack of articulation, the attribute must be modified (replaced by, idealized) into an exact one if it is to be incorporated into a scientific theory the underlying logic of which is L or indeed any logic which satisfies the requirement of extensional definiteness.

The indefiniteness of propositions is an obvious consequence of the inexactness of attributes: If an object can with equal correctness be assigned or refused membership in a class, then the proposition that this object belongs to the class can with equal correctness be judged to be true or judged to be false. Such indefinite or neutral propositions, though by no means foreign to commonsense, violate the requirement of propositional definiteness which is characteristic of L and other logical systems and of the scientific theories embedded in them. If an indefinite proposition is to be accommodated into a scientific theory of the type described, the proposition must be modified (replaced by, idealized) into a definite proposition.

The inexactness of some attributes in respect of which objects are equal or indistinguishable involves the non-transitive character of the equality or indistinguishability in question. This was clearly and emphatically pointed out by Poincaré.[2] Consider for example equality in weight as apprehended either by our unaided senses or by our senses aided by a balance (or some other instrument). However finely calibrated our balance may be, it is always possible to find three objects, say, a, b, c, such that a balances b, b balances c, but a does not balance c. To deny this possibility for every triple of objects having weight is to assume the possibility of an infinitely sensitive balance. The relation of mathematical equality and of quantitative equality assumed in any scientific theory is, of course, transitive. If, therefore a statement of a commonsense (operational, perceptual) equality is to be incorporated into such a

---

[1] For some purposes it is useful to supplement the distinction between exact and inexact attributes by a further distinction between internally exact and internally inexact attributes (see *Experience and Theory*, ch. IV, §4).

[2] See, e.g., *La Science et l'Hypothèse* (Paris, 1912), ch. II.

theory the non-transitive relation of indistinguishability must be modified into a transitive equality relation.

What has been said about axiomatic theories embedded in L applies
with obvious modifications also to non-axiomatic theories which are so
embedded. In such theories the deduction of a state-description from a
conjunction of hypotheses and another state-description can, as in the
case of axiomatic theories, be represented by the schema: $(s_1$ and $A)$ $\vdash_L s_2$,
provided that the schema is interpreted in a different manner. The
symbol '$\vdash_L$' of deducibility by means of L is interpreted as before, i.e.
in particular as subjecting the premises and the conclusion to the requirements of definite truth-values, exact attributes, and transitive
equality relations. The conjunction of hypotheses A, however, is not a
conjunction of axioms. Indeed in many non-axiomatic theoretical
systems—whether or not they deserve the name of a theory—the stock
of hypotheses and even the vocabulary may be too fluid to invite or to
permit axiomatization. But in so far as these systems contain deductive
stretches their underlying logic may be, and often is, L.

In emphasizing certain differences between L and the logical structure
of commonsense thinking we certainly do not exhibit this structure
completely. But it is possible to construct a logic L^* which on the one
hand allows for exact and inexact attributes and for truth-functionally
definite and indefinite propositions and which on the other hand represents a generalization of L in the sense that it reduces to L when only
exact attributes and definite propositions are admitted. L^* is not *the*
logic of commonsense, but a logic which focuses attention on features of
commonsense thinking which L excludes. The method which leads from
L to the more liberal L^* is also available in widening I into an intuitionist
logic admitting exact and inexact attributes as well as definite and indefinite propositions. How it is used in the case of L, I, and other logical
theories is explained in the Appendix.

*On the categorial structure of theoretical as compared with commonsense
thinking*

In contrasting and comparing the categorial structure of scientific and
commonsense thinking it is useful to pay particular attention to three
features which are prominent in scientific thinking. They are mathematization which, though it also occurs outside scientific thinking, is
mainly limited to it; deductive abstraction which occurs in all theorizing
and not only in scientific theorizing; and theoretical innovation which,
though peculiar neither to scientific nor to non-scientific thinking, is
more characteristic of theorizing than of commonsense thinking.

Mathematization, as was briefly illustrated in our example of classical
dynamics, consists in assuming that particulars, whatever their categorization into maximal kinds, are (or are associated with) quantities,

the relations between which are isomorphic with relations between numbers or other mathematical entities. Mathematization thus presupposes some prior mathematical theory or theories and therefore the acknowledgment of one or more maximal kinds of mathematical particulars. However, in order to consider the rôle of mathematization in scientific theorizing, it is not necessary to ask and answer the ontological questions as to whether mathematical particulars are independent, as was held, e.g. by Plato, or dependent as was held, e.g. by Aristotle; whether, say, 'being a natural number' logically implies (in some logic) the constitutive attribute 'being a member of an actual infinity', or whether this attribute is empty; whether a mathematical entity is individuated by any attribute which it alone possesses or whether in the case of mathematical entities—as in the case of some others—it is proper to distinguish mere identification from individuation.

The comparison between the quantitative, 'mathematized' particulars, classes, and relations of theoretical thinking and their commonsense counterparts, if any, proceeds on the same lines as the comparison between the logical structure of theoretical thinking and commonsense. The theoretical structure is once again transparent and capable of unambiguous, axiomatic formulation, whereas the corresponding commonsense structure is relatively opaque and inaccessible to sharp formulation. One of the first formulations of the theoretical principles governing the representation of quantities as multiples and fractions of a unit, the addition of quantities and their multiplication by a number, is due to Helmholtz.[1] Without going into details it is clear that, for example, theoretical addition differs from physical addition (e.g. of weights, lengths, durations) by its freedom from any limitation in the number or size of the added quantities. Again theoretical addition is in a non-temporal and non-spatial sense commutative, whereas the results of physical addition may depend on the spatio-temporal arrangement of the added quantities.

When the results of experiment and observation are formulated in terms of functional relations between quantities arranged in a continuous order (i.e. an order isomorphic with the continuum of real numbers), there can be no question that very radical idealizations of commonsense thinking are involved. The contrast between an observed continuous process or region and the ideal structures described in, say, Dedekind's theory of the continuum is indeed striking. One is not describing or measuring an observed continuous process or region when, among other things, one postulates that it consists of phases or elements such that between any two of them their lies an infinite number of further

---

[1] See 'Zählen und Messen—erkenntnisstheoretisch betrachtet' in Gesammelte Abhandlungen, vol. 3 (Leipzig, 1895).

phases or elements, and that the infinity in question is non-denumerable, i.e. in a precise sense 'greater' than the set of all integers.

The structural constraints imposed in conformity with one or more branches of pure mathematics (usually classical mathematics) upon commonsense thinking by the principles of quantitative reasoning, affect all scientific theories in and through which inferences are drawn from measurements. Only the principles of logic (usually classical logic) are wider in scope. With the general, logico-mathematical modifications of commonsense thinking which account, as it were, for the overall structure of scientific theories, there are coupled the special modifications of commonsense thinking, namely deductive abstraction and theoretical innovation, which vary from theory to theory. If the logico-mathematical modifications can be compared to a general tightening of the conceptual net of commonsense, then deductive abstraction might be compared to a removal of some of its strands, and theoretical innovation to the addition of new ones. Both can again be briefly and clearly illustrated by reference to classical dynamics.

The concept of a particle, as understood in that theory, provides an obvious example of deductive abstraction. It is not just the concept of a very small material object, but a considerably attenuated version of it. More precisely, whereas a small material object possesses not only a certain position and a certain momentum (mass times velocity), but also a certain colour and temperature, a particle of classical dynamics possesses only position and momentum. 'Being a material object of any size' logically implies 'Being a material object which has some degree of heat'. 'Being a particle', on the other hand, logically implies 'not having any degree of heat'—since otherwise the explanation of heat in terms of the energy of moving particles would be viciously circular.[1] Examples of theoretical innovation in classical dynamics are the concept of energy and, possibly, such concepts as 'momentary velocity' and 'momentary acceleration'. Yet it might be argued that at least the last two can also be accounted for by deductive abstraction coupled with the constraints arising from the employment of the mathematical theory of real numbers.

It is, however, of little importance where the lines are drawn between the various ways in which theoretical and commonsense thinking differ from each other. This applies not only to the distinction between deductive abstraction and theoretical innovation, but also to the distinction between general mathematical and special non-mathematical modifications, for example to the question whether statistical theory should be regarded as a general mathematical theory or as a special

[1] The 'cutting off' of the logical relation between the attributes of being a particle and of possessing a degree of heat is one reason for my having chosen the term 'deductive abstraction'.

physical theory concerned with mass-phenomena. Even the distinction between general logical and general mathematical modifications is not immutably fixed, since the theory of equality could, and sometimes is, considered as part of mathematics rather than of elementary logic. What is important here is the contrast between commonsense and theories; and this is unaffected by such redrawing of the boundaries.

On the joint employment of commonsense and theoretical attributes and particulars in scientific thinking

The state-descriptions, say s_1 and s_2, of an axiomatic or non-axiomatic scientific theory which employs the usual logico-mathematical apparatus for its deductions are, as we have seen, not descriptions of observational or experimental findings but idealizations of them. This insight is at least as old as Plato's theory of Forms, even though it is independent of the Platonic metaphysics. It finds expression in some of Galileo Galilei's philosophical *obiter dicta* and has recently been expressed by Heisenberg, who holds that through the 'process of precise definition and idealization' of the concepts of natural language their 'immediate connection with reality is lost'; that the idealized concepts 'still correspond very closely to reality in that part of nature which has been the object of research' but that 'the correspondence may be lost in other parts containing other groups of phenomena'.[1]

The contact between s_1 and s_2 on the one hand, and experience on the other, which has been lost as a result of the general and special modifications of a natural language (in return for a great gain in inferential efficiency), is re-established by *identifying* the theoretical statements s_1 and s_2 and their constituent concepts with ordinary, empirical statements and their constituent ordinary, empirical concepts. One should be quite clear about the nature of this identification. It is not the recognition of an identity but the recognition or assumption that s_1 and s_2 can *within limited contexts and for limited purposes* be regarded *as if* they were identical with corresponding empirical statements, say e_1 and e_2, which in any unidealized, natural language express actual or possible experimental or observational findings. How to demarcate the limits of this identification is itself an empirical question which can be answered only by observation and experiment and by comparing them with successful or unsuccessful predictions. The general principle, which guides the identification of unmodified, empirical with idealized, theoretical statements, might be called 'the principle of the negligibility of the neglected'. It expresses the obvious requirement that if in a certain context an empirical and an ideal concept or statement are identified, those features which are neglected by the identification should in its context be negligible.

[1] *Physics and Philosophy* (London, 1959), p. 171.

Any branch of inquiry in which predictions are made by identifying theoretical concepts and statements with corresponding commonsense ones might be called 'double-layered'. All quantitative natural and social sciences are double-layered since they employ at the very least both the non-transitive notion of perceptual and the transitive notion of mathematical equality. Even seemingly descriptive and taxonomical sciences may be double-layered, e.g. if they employ both inexact commonsense and modified exact classifications. History, on the other hand, is single-layered. In its traditional form, it tries to describe sequences of events as they have occurred, and has no use for a simplified ideal world as described by an axiomatic or less strictly organized theory. Those reformers who from time to time propose that history be pursued after the fashion of the natural sciences as a rule also propose a new name for the new subject, such as 'social physics', 'sociology', 'social anthropology', and the rest.

Because of the double-layered character at most, if not quite all, scientific thinking one must not, while attending to the structure of its theories, ignore its bottom layer, i.e. those commonsense concepts and propositions with which some of the ideal concepts and propositions of this or that scientific theory have to be identified, if the theory is to be of any use in prediction.[1] Indeed, even regions of commonsense thought which, like traditional morality, religion or aesthetic sensibility, do not form the bottom layer of any two-layered scientific thinking may have to be considered, if their influence on all commonsense and, therefore, on the bottom layer of scientific thinking becomes evident.

The question of ontological primacy
Having distinguished between the logical structure of scientific and commonsense thinking, i.e. between L and L^* (I and I^* or any other pair of theories of which one member is 'unstarred' and the other 'starred'), we must once again ask and answer the question which of them is primary and which secondary. As in the case of the contrast between the logical structure of factual and constructive thinking, i.e. between L and I (or L^* and I^* or any other pair of theories of which one member is factual and the other constructive), both answers can be justified. One may hold with Plato or Descartes that definiteness and distinctness are necessary conditions of 'genuine' knowledge and that perceptual propositions and their underlying starred logic are merely a preliminary and auxiliary stage preceding rational propositions with their underlying unstarred logic. On such a view L or some other unstarred logic is the primary logic. Mathematics, the Platonic and

----

[1] For a more detailed analysis of the function of theoretical and commonsense propositions in scientific prediction, see *Experience and Theory*, ch. XII.

Cartesian prototype of knowledge, is certainly embedded in L or, at least in an unstarred logic.

One may, on the other hand, hold with Locke and other empiricists that the prototype of knowledge is perceptual; and that since perceptual knowledge is embedded in L^* or some other starred logic, L, or any other unstarred logic, is a mere auxiliary fiction. From our point of view, which emphasizes external corrigibility rather than internal incorrigibility, it is more important to understand the relation between L and L^* and other corresponding unstarred and starred logical systems, than to award the title of ontological primacy to one of them. This does not, of course, mean that the rationalist's or empiricist's acceptance of one logic as primary is a mistake or that it is of no consequence to him.

A similar problem about the ontological primacy of 'scientific objects', such as Newtonian particles, over 'ordinary material things', such as stones, is frequently raised and discussed with some heat. Since the problem is empirically undecidable, the proper logico-epistemological attitude is again one of tolerant impartiality. This does not mean that a person who shares this point of view may not adopt one of these ontological positions in his own thinking and acting or that he may not endeavour to support it by arguments. Such arguments need be no less rational for being pragmatic and directed *ad hominem*, especially if they are recognized as such.[1]

To distinguish between the logical and categorial structure of commonsense thinking on the one hand, and of theoretical thinking on the other is not to deny their mutual interaction. The situation here bears some analogies to the interaction between factual and constructive thinking. Just as objects and propositions of constructive thinking become after suitable modifications objects and propositions of factual thinking and *vice versa*, so the objects and propositions of commonsense thinking enter, again after suitable modifications, the sphere of theoretical thinking and *vice versa*. To what I have called the 'fact-construction cycle' there corresponds what might be called the 'commonsense-theory cycle'. The modifications involved in the latter are fairly obvious. On entering into theoretical thinking commonsense propositions are subjected to the constraints of L (I or another unstarred logic) and of mathematization, they are attenuated by deductive abstraction and enriched by theoretical innovation. When, on the other hand, theoretical objects and propositions—such as the notion of a field of force or the law of the conservation of energy—are received into commonsense, the logical requirements of L (I or some other unstarred logic) are replaced by the looser ones of L^* (I^* or some other starred logic), the constraints imposed by mathematization are dropped and the original logical relations enriched in some ways and reduced in others. Even without an extensive study of the commonsense-theory cycle, it should be clear that the traffic between commonsense and theory is not one-sided: commonsense assumptions lie below many a layer of theoretical thought, and accepted or discarded bits of theory are hidden in much that is considered sheer, undiluted commonsense.

Chapter V

The purpose of the preceding chapters was to exhibit differences within, rather than between, categorial frameworks. Where distinctions between categorial frameworks were made, they concerned mainly the issue of ontological priority. Thus the distinction between factual and constructive thinking in no way implies that one and the same person or group of persons may not in their thinking employ both L and I, or both factual and constructive maximal kinds; but only that such joint employment may for different persons or groups of persons be coupled with different answers as to which logical theory is primary and which secondary, and which maximal kinds are independent and which dependent. Analogous remarks apply to the distinction between common-sense and theoretical thinking.

Henceforth the emphasis will shift from differences within, to differences between, categorial frameworks especially those which stem from divergent interpretations and idealizations of a common stock of acknowledged particulars, attributes and propositions. The tasks of the present chapter are first, to explain and to illustrate the nature of divergent interpretations and idealizations; second, to exhibit their rôle in giving rise to different metaphysical and other *a priori* principles; lastly, to indicate the function of these principles as standards of explanation and intelligibility.

Divergent interpretations

Earlier in this essay (p. 2) I have, without any attempt at justification, assumed that categorial frameworks may differ from each other because a preconceptual or unconceptualized experience may in several possible ways be differentiated into particulars and attributes; and because even after their apprehension as separate, particulars can be grouped in several possible ways into natural classes. Both these assumptions are also made by some anthropologists and linguists,[1] the first as a highly speculative hypothesis, the second as a more or less straightforward

---

[1] See F. de Saussure, *Cours de Linguistique Génerale* (Paris, 1949) ch. IV, and C. Lévi-Strauss, *La Pensée Sauvage* (Paris, 1962).

empirical generalization. Yet even if these assumptions were false and if all human beings shared a common initial stock of particulars and attributes, there would still be room for categorial divergence. This is especially obvious if we assume that the particulars and attributes are perceptual.

Let us then suppose that a person, a group of persons or even everybody employs a stock of attributes in 'describing' what he perceives, remembers as having perceived or imagines to be perceivable, and consider the possibility of divergently 'interpreting' what is described. The distinction between describing and interpreting is not meant to be absolute or to imply the possibility of separating pure and unalloyed descriptive attributes from attributes which combine descriptive and interpretative elements. Of the statements that the same perceptual object is a white piece of paper with black marks, a type-written notice, and a summons to a meeting, the second is more interpretative than the first, the third more interpretative than the second. But the applicability of the relation 'more interpretative' does not imply the applicability of 'absolutely most interpretative' or of 'absolutely least interpretative', i.e. 'absolutely descriptive'.

It is possible to find, or to form, pairs of attributes which do not differ in their perceptual content, but differ in the degree to which they are interpretative. Examples are (a) 'x is a table participating in the Platonic Form of the Table', 'x is a table'; (b) 'x is regularly followed by y as its effect', 'x is regularly followed by y'. The second pair plays a central rôle in the philosophy of Hume who from the perceptual indistinguishability of the two attributes infers the emptiness of the concept of causality. That this inference is not valid was argued by Kant whose theory of *a priori* concepts and judgments was partly prompted by his examination of Hume's analysis of causality. Yet although he recognized that the two attributes in our last example differ in interpretative degree, he did not consider the problem of interpretative divergence. The following definitions will be useful in tackling this problem.

I shall say that two attributes, P and Q, have the same perceptual content or are 'co-ostensive' if, and only if, to every instance of one of the attributes there corresponds an instance of the other from which it is perceptually indistinguishable; or, alternatively if, and only if, there is no perceptual criterion for deciding whether an instance of one of them is, or is not, also an instance of the other. And I shall say that of the two co-ostensive attributes P and Q, P is 'interpretative of' Q—and therefore more interpretative than Q—if, and only if, the possession of P by an object logically implies, but is not logically implied by, the possession by the object of Q. If the unilateral logical implication is defined in terms of the classical elementary logic L we may say more precisely that P is interpretative of the co-ostensive Q if, and only if, the form 'If

$P(x)$ then $Q(x)$' (but not its converse) is valid in L, i.e. if $\vdash_L (\forall x)(P(x) \rightarrow Q(x))$ but not $\vdash_L (\forall x)(Q(x) \rightarrow P(x))$.

Intuitively speaking, if the possession of P by an object logically implies, but is not implied by, the possession of the co-ostensive Q by the object, then there must exist a non-perceptual attribute, say R, such that the possession of P by an object logically implies, *and* is logically implied by, the possession of both P and R by the object. This intuition is borne out by the following metatheorem of L according to which if $\vdash_L (\forall x)(P(x) \rightarrow Q(x))$ then there exists an R such that $\vdash_L (\forall x)(P(x) \leftrightarrow (Q(x) \wedge R(x)))$. The attribute $R(x)$ is the non-perceptual difference between $P(x)$ and $Q(x)$; and conjoining it with $Q(x)$ turns the unilateral logical implication into a bilateral logical implication or logical equivalence. In the first of our examples the non-perceptual difference R between the two co-ostensive attributes is 'x participates in the Platonic Form of the Table'. In the second example R is the attribute 'x CAUSES y', where 'CAUSES' is that relation whose applicability turns a merely regular into a causal sequence.

For our purpose it is fortunately not necessary to develop a method for stratifying the attributes employed by a thinker or group of thinkers into interpretative levels since even the stratification of co-ostensive attributes may become rather involved. Thus if Q, P_1, and P_2 are co-ostensive and if P_1 and P_2 are both interpretative of the same Q it does not follow that one of them is interpretative of the other. They may even be mutually incompatible. The stratification into interpretative levels of attributes which—like 'x participates in the Platonic Form of the Table' or 'x causes y'—are not co-ostensive is even more complex. To exhibit the complexity would not be illuminating, while to simplify it would require some rather unrealistic assumptions.[1]

The possibility of co-ostensive and yet mutually exclusive attributes and the consequent mutual exclusiveness of their non-perceptual or *a priori* ingredients account for fairly radical differences between categorial frameworks. The presence of such *a priori* attributes as 'participates in a Platonic Form' or 'causes' among the constitutive attributes of a maximal kind does not only affect its members but also their relations to other kinds. Thus one's conception of material objects as participating in Platonic Forms, some of which have mathematical and none of which have perceptual characteristics, will, among other things, affect one's conception of the relation between pure mathematics and its 'application' to perceptual and physical objects.

In a more detailed study of interpretative attributes the following three types would deserve special attention as characteristic of most— possibly all—categorial frameworks so far employed. These are attri-

---

[1] For an approach of the latter type, see *Conceptual Thinking* (Cambridge 1955, New York, 1959), ch. XVII.

butes which, roughly speaking, serve the transformation of a plurality of particulars into a unified particular of a new kind; attributes which serve the transformation of private particulars into public particulars; and attributes which serve the transformation of transient into permanent particulars. A few remarks about each of these types will have to suffice.

To start with 'unifying attributes', as one might call interpretative attributes of the first type, we consider a set of perceptual attributes $\{Q_1 \ldots Q_n\}$ each of which is characteristic of distinct particulars. An attribute P is a unifying attribute interpretative of the set $\{Q_1 \ldots Q_n\}$ if, and only if, (i) P, as applied to one particular, is co-ostensive with $\{Q_1 \ldots Q_n\}$, each member of the set being applied to a different particular, and (ii) The applicability of P to one particular logically implies, but is not logically implied by, the applicability of $\{Q_1 \ldots Q_n\}$ to n distinct particulars (each instantiating one attribute of the set). The *a priori* ingredient by which P differs from the co-ostensive $\{Q_1 \ldots Q_n\}$ is the attribute of being a substratum of which $Q_1 \ldots Q_n$ are jointly characteristic or in which they jointly inhere.

The classic example of a unifying attribute is the notion of a physical object in the restricted sense of a substratum in which such attributes as are separately characteristic of distinct impressions jointly inhere. However, the notion or the various notions of a physical object are not the only attributes unifying distinct impressions into unified particulars. The unifying function may, for example, also be fulfilled by different notions of natural event, situation, process, etc. Another example of a unifying attribute is the notion of a society, provided that it is conceived as co-ostensive with the set of attributes characteristic of the plurality of persons belonging to it. It is worth noting that the transformation of pluralities into unities by means of unifying attributes may be iterated. Thus the attributes of separate physical objects may be regarded as inhering in one material substratum, the attributes of separate men or societies in one superhuman substratum, etc.

As regards attributes which serve the interpretative transformation of perceived particulars into public and of transient into permanent particulars the situation is quite simple. The attribute of being public, both in the weak sense of being perceivable by everybody and in the strong sense of existing independently of being perceived, is clearly non-perceptual. It is logically impossible to perceive a particular's perceivability by others or to perceive its existence independently of perceiving it. Thus if Q is any perceptual attribute and if R is the attribute of being a public object it follows that (i) (Q and R) is co-ostensive with Q and (ii) that (Q and R) logically implies, but is not logically implied by Q. 'Q and R' is interpretative of 'Q' and to apply the former attribute to an instance of the latter is to transform it into a public particular.

The attribute of being permanent, both in the weak sense of persisting when unperceived and in the stronger senses of so persisting for a long or for an unlimited time, is also clearly non-perceptual. To adjoin it to any perceptual attribute is thus again to form an attribute interpretative of the former. To apply the interpretative attribute to an instance of its interpreted component is to transform a transient particular into a permanent particular. Many notions of external object or external phenomenon contain interpretative attributes of all the three types mentioned as non-perceptual ingredients.

The interpretation of a plurality of particulars as a new particular, of perceived particulars as public and as permanent particulars is not restricted to factual thinking. For example, in the case of our unifying attribute P which is interpretative of the set $\{Q_1 \ldots Q_n\}$, the application of one or more Q's to one or more appropriate particulars may depend on the exercise of options and thus become the subject-matter of practical and, therefore, of constructive thinking. Reference to options certainly enters the definitions of those species of material objects which are defined as materials or instruments; and it is arguable that even the genus 'material object' as used in the Indo–European languages includes such a reference.

Divergent idealizations

Idealization, the rôle of which in science has been discussed in chapter IV under the heading of deductive unification, deductive abstraction, and theoretical innovation, is not restricted to scientific theories. It manifests itself also in theories which, like theology, are not scientific or which, like non-theoretical simplifying generalizations about people, situations or developments, lack the systematic unification which is characteristic of theorizing. Apart from a possible border-region between interpretation and idealization the two function in a clearly different manner. To interpret a description is to add non-descriptive elements to it, e.g. when we interpret a sequence of situations as causal; to idealize a description is to modify the description itself, e.g. when we replace a statement about a perceptual triangle by a statement about an Euclidean one. In order to clarify the notion of idealization in theoretical and non-theoretical contexts I shall, as in the case of the notion of interpretation, try to characterize the locutions 'P is an idealization of Q' and 'P_1 is a stronger idealization of Q than is P_2'.

Let us say that P_1 is a first order idealization of Q if, and only if, (i) Q is a more or less highly interpretative attribute of perceptual objects; (ii) The applicability of P_1 to an object neither logically implies, nor is logically implied by, the applicability to it of Q; (iii) For some specific purposes, but not for all, (i.e. for a proper subset of the purposes) for which Q is used P_1 may be identified with Q. Similarly, P_2 is a

5

second order idealization of Q if, and only if, (i) There is (employed by the thinker or group of thinkers with whom we are concerned) a first order idealization P_1 of Q; (ii) The applicability of P_2 neither logically implies, nor is logically implied by, the applicability of Q; (iii) For some specific purposes, but not for all, for which P_1 is used P_2 may be identified with P_1. The definition for the nth idealization of Q ($n > 2$) is obvious.

The higher the order of idealization the further removed are the idealizing attributes from the idealized ones and the narrower is the class of specific purposes for which they are used. In scientific thinking the remoteness from perception and the restriction of purposes served is, as we have seen, well worth the advantages gained: scientific theories in conjunction with commonsense concepts serve the specific purposes of predicting and controlling areas of nature more efficiently than commonsense unaided by theories. It is not equally clear that extra-scientific idealizations, e.g. those that are employed in religious, theological or aesthetic thinking, serve their specific purposes better than the many-purpose concepts of which they are idealizations. Yet it seems a reasonable conjecture that a desire for this kind of increased efficiency is the rationale of many, if not all, idealizations.

The prospect of stratifying the idealizing attributes used by a person into levels of idealization is even less promising than the prospect of stratifying the interpretative attributes used by him. Thus the sequence $Q, P_1, \ldots, P_n$ which, starting with the more or less interpretative attribute Q increasingly idealizes this attribute, depends on the manner in which the class of purposes for which Q is used is gradually restricted. Another such sequence will correspond to another gradual narrowing down of these purposes. Again attributes belonging to different sequences may for specific purposes be identifiable with each other. Lastly the route leading from Q to P_n may lead through different intermediate concepts. An exception are various set-theoretical attributes which result from successive syntheses of pluralities of ideal particulars into higher unities, e.g. 'plurality of ideal particulars', 'set of ideal particulars', 'plurality of sets of ideal particulars', 'set of sets of ideal particulars', etc. However, for our purpose, which is to show the possibility of divergent idealizations, it is not necessary to attempt a stratification of these or any other idealizing attributes.

What is called the 'application' of idealizing attributes to perceptual objects must be distinguished from the applications of other attributes to these objects. This is particularly obvious when the idealizing attributes are mathematical. When an astronomer engaged on measuring the distances between three stars judges them to form a triangle, he is not asserting that the figure formed by them is, in addition to being a physical triangle, also a Euclidean or a non-Euclidean triangle or both.

He is asserting that for the purpose in hand the physical triangle can be treated as if it were either a Euclidean triangle or else a non-Euclidean triangle or that it can be treated indifferently as one or the other. This indirect, *as-if-* application of geometrical and other idealizing attributes differs clearly from the straightforward application of physical attributes to physical objects.

Idealizing and interpretative attributes may be related in a variety of ways. It is in particular noteworthy that there is a simple and uniform procedure for transforming any first order idealizing attribute into a non-perceptual ingredient of an interpretative attribute. Let $Q(x)$ be a more or less interpretative attribute and $D(x)$ a first order idealization of it, so that $Q(x)$ is for certain specific purposes s identifiable with $D(x)$. If we now form the attribute 'being a Q and (thus) for the purpose s identifiable with a D', briefly ' $Q(x) \underset{s}{\approx} D(x)$', then $((Q(x)$ and $(Q(x) \underset{s}{\approx} D(x)))$ is interpretative of $Q(x)$ and contains $(Q(x) \underset{s}{\approx} D(x))$ as a non-perceptual ingredient. For clearly (i) $((Q(x)$ and $(Q(x) \underset{s}{\approx} D(x)))$ and $Q(x)$ are co-ostensive and (ii) the applicability to an object of the former attribute logically implies, but is not logically implied by, the applicability of the latter attribute to the object. The following triplet of attributes may serve as an illustration: $Q(x) = $ 'x is a physical object'; $D(x) = $ 'x is a stable, isolated system of molecules in a certain arrangement'; $(Q(x) \underset{s}{\approx} D(x)) = $ 'x is a physical object and for the purposes s identifiable with a stable, isolated system of molecules in a certain arrangement'.

While thus every first order idealizing attribute can in a simple and uniform manner be transformed into a non-perceptual ingredient of an interpretative attribute, the converse does not seem to be the case. Consider for example once again (a version of) the interpretative attribute 'x is a material object' which, conceived as interpretative of 'x appears to me to be a material object', contains among its non-perceptual ingredients 'x is a public object' and 'x is a substratum of perceptual attributes'. Although each of these non-perceptual attributes might be regarded as the result of idealizing a perceptual attribute, the transformations do not seem to follow any uniform procedure. In any case, the possibility of such transformations—be they unilateral or bilateral, uniform or heterogeneous—does not deprive the distinction between interpretative and idealizing attributes of its justification.

The non-perceptual ingredients of interpretative attributes and their first- or higher-order idealizations are not necessarily the only non-perceptual attributes employed in factual or constructive thinking. I see no reason for insisting that concepts such as 'God', 'Soul', 'destiny' are the result of idealizing interpretative concepts—especially as the only kinds of idealization described in some detail have been deductive unification and deductive abstraction. A more taxonomical approach might, among other kinds of transformation, consider the transition from attributes admitting of degrees to their perfections, e.g. from 'knowledgeable' to 'omniscient' or from 'powerful' to 'omnipotent'.

The possibility and the historical fact of divergent interpretations and idealizations would explain the possible and actual variety of categorial frameworks—even if all people were endowed with a common initial stock of attributes. It might at first sight seem that there is much more scope in the formation of idealizing than in the formation of interpretative attributes. But this impression is easily dispelled if we remember that every first order idealization of an interpretative attribute Q can be transformed into an *a priori* ingredient of a new interpretative attribute which is interpretative of Q.

Divergent interpretations and idealizations in metaphysics

We have seen (in chapter II) that the constitutive and individuating principles associated with a categorial framework are internally incorrigible, but externally corrigible. This double-faced character of framework-principles is independent of the degree to which its constitutive and individuating attributes are interpretative or idealizing. Even if one quite unrealistically assumed that interpretation and idealization play no part in the formation of attributes and that the variety of classificatory schemes and categorizations is due solely to alternative methods of differentiating a total experience into particulars and attributes, the framework-principles would still be internally incorrigible and externally corrigible. An example of such a framework-principle might be provided by a categorial framework F with a maximal kind W, say *visibilia*, of which 'being coloured' is a constitutive attribute. The conjunction of the existential proposition that W is not empty and of the logical proposition that the applicability of W to an object logically implies the applicability of 'coloured' to it, is then a constitutive principle of F. It is not also a constitutive principle of any and every categorial framework since there clearly are categorial frameworks in which W is not a maximal kind.

It is, however, not surprising that Kant and most other metaphysicians and epistemologists have been chiefly interested in constitutive and individuating attributes which are non-perceptual or contain non-perceptual ingredients and in the framework-principles corresponding to such attributes. For it is by means of interpretative attributes, especially those that interpret pluralities into new unities, and by means of idealizing attributes, especially those that are in certain contexts identifiable with interpretative attributes, that intercategorial connections are made and categorial frameworks rendered more flexible for

specific purposes such as scientific prediction.[1] This function of interpretation and idealization must, however, be distinguished from their
contribution to the actual and possible variety of different categorial
frameworks.

Since not only Aristotle and Kant, but all metaphysicians *qua* metaphysicians, pay much attention to categorial frameworks, any demarcation of metaphysics must pay serious attention to them. Whatever else
it may be, metaphysics aims at the exhibition of implicitly accepted
categorial frameworks, at their critical examination and, sometimes,
also at their modification. The modification may be so drastic as to
amount to the speculative proposal of a wholly new categorial framework. An example is Leibniz's rejection of physical atomism in every
form and his proposal of an entirely new categorial framework in which
physical atoms are replaced by spiritual atoms or monads.

Such a delimitation of metaphysics receives additional support from
attempts at characterizing the class of metaphysical principles. The
following characteristics are often put forward: (i) Metaphysical
principles are non-empirical in the sense that their acceptance or rejection does not depend on experiment or observation. (ii) They are not
logically true in the sense of being substitution-instances of logical
principles. (Aristotle and other metaphysicians regard the principles
themselves as both logical and metaphysical.) (iii) They are comprehensive in the sense that they are applicable either to all entities or at least
to the entities of one category or maximal kind. (iv) They are 'prior to
experience' in the sense of *somehow* determining the structure of
experience, rather than being determined by it. Admitting the vagueness
of these conditions, especially of the last, we must, I think, also
admit that if they are satisfied at all, they are satisfied by framework-
principles.

When applied to framework-principles the locutions 'prior to experience' and '*a priori*' tend to obscure important distinctions one of
which concerns the difference between internal and external incorrigibility. Another distinction, which follows from the preceding discussion of interpretative and idealizing attributes, concerns the difference between the perceptual and the non-perceptual ingredients, if any,
of the constitutive and individuating attributes occurring in the framework-principles of a categorial framework *F*. The non-perceptual
ingredients of the interpretative attributes of *F* and the idealizations of
such attributes are, if we like to put it this way, the (or among the) *a
priori* concepts of *F*. But this does not mean that they are the *a priori*
concepts of any and every categorial framework. Kant not only con-
flated the internal incorrigibility of framework-principles with external

incorrigibility, but also regarded the non-perceptual attributes of his categorial framework as common to all.

In classifying framework-principles as metaphysical I do not wish to imply that they exhaust the class of all metaphysical propositions or even the narrower class of what might be called 'categorial principles'. Without attempting too sharp a demarcation we might reasonably count the following types of proposition as categorial principles: (i) Framework-principles, i.e. constitutive and individuating principles. (ii) 'Transcategorial' principles, defining the constitution of any entity whatsoever. Examples would be on the one hand the principles of the logic underlying the categorial framework in question, on the other the principle of sufficient reason, the principle that any entity whatsoever is either simple or consists of simple constituents, or the contradictories of these principles. (iii) 'Metacategorial' principles expressing common features of the categorial principles of a categorial framework (e.g. that its constitutive attributes are non-perceptual or contain nonperceptual ingredients); expressing relations between framework principles (e.g. that every member of the category of material objects 'participates' in a member of the category of Platonic Forms); expressing limitations of framework principles (e.g. the compatibility of all framework principles with the dogmas of a certain religion). (iv) Logical consequences of propositions belonging to one or more of the preceding types.

The propositions of types (i)–(iv) express assumptions made by the person employing the categorial framework of which the propositions are characteristic. To each of these propositions there corresponds a heuristic maxim which enjoins one to conduct oneself, in particular to theorize, as if the proposition were true. This assertion would not be worth making if it were not for the need to point out that its converse need not be true. While all categorial principles correspond to very general heuristic maxims, it is quite possible to accept a heuristic maxim which is not, as it were, backed by a categorial principle. A person who does not accept the principle that every event has a cause, or that every event has a purpose, may yet have good or bad reasons to conduct himself, at least in some contexts, as if every event had a cause, a purpose, or both.

What has been said about the rôle of interpretation and idealization in the formation of constitutive and individuating attributes and the acceptance of the corresponding framework-principles carries over to all categorial principles with obvious minor qualifications. The difference between the logical and categorial structure of factual thinking on the one hand and of constructive thinking on the other does not affect this rôle. There is, moreover, no scarcity of detailed examples. Apart from inconsistencies and other mistakes, treatises on metaphysics or on the foundations of one or more sciences propound competing systems of categorial principles, of which at most one but possibly none, is true; as well as analyses, modifications or proposals of categorial principles which are characteristic of one or more different categorial frameworks or types of them.

Categorial principles and explanation

The differences between categorial frameworks manifest themselves not only in their users' explicit metaphysical beliefs, but also in their conception of what constitutes a satisfactory explanation. Accepting an explanation of something, say, X that is to be explained, involves believing a proposition g. The proposition g is for a person the explanation of X if, and only if, the person believes g and does not regard X as unintelligible, but would regard it so if he did not believe g. The proposition g is for a person an explanation of X if, and only if, g is one of a set of propositions such that if he believes any one of them without the others, it is the explanation of X. If, for example, I saw a horse beside my writing desk and did not believe any of a number of propositions tracing its journey from a more likely place to my room, I should regard its appearance at my desk as unexplained, though not necessarily as unexplainable.

In our definition of an explanation that which is to be explained need not be a proposition. However, this circumstance is of little importance since the X that is to be explained is always to some extent expressible by a proposition. What is more important about the definition is that it is meant to be wide enough to cover every kind of explanation and not, for example, only scientific, theological, historical, or magical explanation. The proposition g which explains X may be compound and X may be a more or less complex combination of items. The set of propositions which a person regards, or would regard, as explaining some X cannot usually be enumerated. But it is obviously not the same for everybody.

The difference between what persons with more or less different intellectual backgrounds regard as an explanation does not simply lie in those attributes which, like the relations of magical, teleological or natural causation have an obvious explanatory function, but rather in the whole conceptual system to which they belong. Thus, the application of any obviously explanatory relation presupposes a demarcation of its domain and its range (e.g. of the class of causes and the class of effects which may but need not coincide). This demarcation is in turn closely linked with the classification of particulars into maximal kinds, their constitutive and individuating principles and their intercategorial relations.

Again to state a proposition g which is explanatory of X is not always to apply an obviously explanatory relation. In order to see this it is instructive to imagine sequences of situations of which the last is properly described by a statement of the form: 'But then I recognized that g which explained what would otherwise have remained unintelligible' and to take care so to select the sequences that the place of g is taken by as great a variety of propositions as possible. The explanatory propositions will in some cases be classifications or identifications. An otherwise unintelligible event, for example, may become intelligible if a misclassified particular is reclassified as a man or if a misidentified man is correctly identified as Mr. So-and-so.

Yet, however ingeniously one devised these thought-experiments, certain propositions would not be suitable explanatory endings. Which propositions would and which would not be capable of fulfilling this function will depend at least in part on the categorial framework of the person designing the imaginary sequences. Such thought-experiments suggest that if a proposition g is incompatible with the internally incorrigible principles of a categorial framework F, it does not explain anything with respect to F. The suggestion can easily be hardened into a rather trivial proof. If g is recognized as incompatible with the incorrigible principles of F, then the assertion of g amounts to the abandonment of F. And a proposition the assertion of which amounts to the abandonment of F does not explain anything with respect to it. If g is not explanatory with respect to one categorial framework, it may well be explanatory with respect to another. But it cannot be explanatory apart from any categorial framework.

In so far as the compatibility of any proposition g with the internally incorrigible principles of F is a necessary condition of the proposition's explaining anything, these principles represent for the person who employs F not only metaphysical beliefs, but also standards of intelligibility. This does not mean that a person's idea of intelligibility or of what constitutes a satisfactory explanation is exhaustible by these principles. It may include additional desiderata, such as elegance, beauty, and simplicity the sense of which is expressed by means of illustrative examples rather than by clear criteria. A person's idea of intelligibility may further require a balancing of the relative importance of different desiderata and requirements. Lastly it may be exposed to competition from other categorial frameworks which, though considered from the outside only, hold out some promise of accommodating unfamiliar features of the world which cannot without artificiality be explained in familiar ways; or which cast doubt even on familiar explanations of familiar circumstances. But the problem of competition between categorial frameworks and of categorial change generally is best left to a separate chapter.

Chapter VI

It remains to consider some aspects of categorial change and of the competition between categorial frameworks. The present chapter begins briefly comparing the twofold function of categorial frameworks as frameworks of information and of explanation. Next some characteristics and historically important examples of categorial change are briefly described and discussed. The chapter ends with an examination of the ways in which different types of philosophical argument reduce or increase tensions between a categorial framework and its content, and the ways in which they serve the resolution of conflicts between competing categorial frameworks.

Throughout the following discussion I shall carefully avoid two mistaken assumptions against which a clear warning might not be out of place. First, one must not assume that any categorial change is accompanied by philosophical argument since categorial changes may occur in cultures which know no explicit metaphysics. Second, one must not assume that it is possible to indicate necessary and sufficient conditions for the failure or success of a philosophical argument in support of a new categorial framework or in favour of retaining an old one. This assumption comes dangerously near to the conception of a predictive science of categorial change which would enable one to know as yet unknown categorial frameworks and thus to know something before knowing it. A similar claim is also involved in so-called transcendental arguments.

Information and explanation

A proposition is informative for a person in so far as he believes it to be true. It is explanatory for a person if (in the sense defined at the end of the preceding chapter) it renders something intelligible to him. While in accordance with these definitions, any proposition which is explanatory for a person is also informative for him, the converse is not true. Again, a proposition which for a person is both explanatory and informative may cease to be explanatory but remain informative. Thus the information about somebody's death may include a causal explanation which is later rejected as unacceptable. The rejection of the explanation need not involve a categorial change, for example if the rejected causal explanation is replaceable by another. But it may involve a categorial change, for example if all causal explanations are rejected in favour of probabilistic or teleological ones.

The distinction between information and explanation as drawn by—or on behalf of—one person gives rise to the question of shared information and explanation. It seems intuitively plausible that two people with radically different categorial frameworks are more likely to share their information than their explanations. Let g be a proposition expressed in the categorial framework of a person A and h a proposition expressed in the categorial framework of a person B. It is then reasonable to say that g and h have the same informative content for A and B if, and only if, (in so far as) (i) g is informative for A and h is informative for B; (ii) A and B are able to co-operate successfully in every situation in which the success of their co-operation, as it appears to each of them, depends on A's assuming that B will conduct himself as if he believed g and on B's assuming that A will conduct himself as if he believed h. Although this pragmatic notion of common information admits—and stands in need of—elaboration, it is sufficient for our purpose. It covers, in particular, the case where g and h are the same proposition, expressed by the same sentence, in the same language.

Two propositions g and h may have a common informative content for A and B even if g is incompatible with the constitutive and individuating principles of B's categorial framework and if h is incompatible with the constitutive and individuating principles of A's categorial framework. In contrast with this latitude allowed to common information, g and h could not express any explanation common to A and B. For if g is incompatible with the principles of B's categorial framework, then his assertion of g would amount to his abandoning the framework. That is to say that to a person who has not abandoned the framework, g does not explain anything at all. The same holds in the case of h's incompatibility with the principles of A's categorial framework. More briefly, and less precisely, explanation is framework-bound whereas information is not.

We can now characterize, and thereby avoid, two opposite errors which tend to obscure our understanding of categorial change. The first consists in inferring from the true premiss that (Ia) explanation is framework-bound and the false premiss that (II) there is no difference between explanation and information, the false conclusion (IIIa) that information is framework-bound and thus is lost if the constitutive and individuating principles of a categorial framework are replaced by principles with which they are incompatible. The second error consists in inferring from the true premiss that (Ib) information is not framework-bound and the false premiss that (II) there is no difference between explanation and information, the false conclusion (IIIb) that explanation is not framework-bound. The former conclusion tends to support an anthropologism which exaggerates cultural relativity to a point where any understanding of the users of one categorial framework by those of another is completely ruled out. The latter conclusion tends to support a scientism which equates increase of information with improvement of explanation and, consequently, equates the power of science to produce the largest amount of information with a power to produce the best explanations.

Since the general pragmatic definition of common information is admittedly rather crude, it might well seem desirable not to presuppose it in the following examination of categorial change. I shall, in fact, restrict myself to contexts in which any item of common information and any accepted or rejected explanation can be expressed in one and the same natural language, namely ordinary English and its relevant technical extensions.

Some examples of categorial change

Qua answers to the traditional metaphysical questions what maximal kinds there are and what constitutes and individuates them, constitutive and individuating principles are metaphysical propositions. If they are characteristic of one's own categorial framework, their familiarity may make them appear trivial; if of another's radically different categorial framework, their unfamiliarity may make them appear absurd. Hence the frequent complaint that metaphysics is either trivial or absurd. But there are situations when the attempt to accommodate new information into an accepted categorial framework, or even a new look at the information already accommodated, makes familiar principles appear strange and unfamiliar ones plausible. When this happens categorial change may be imminent and philosophical arguments may become relevant in bringing it about or preventing it.

It would be rash to claim any competence in describing the experience of categorial change. One is tempted to compare it to the experience of perceptual change when a manifold, which has hitherto been perceived as one *Gestalt*, is first intermittently and then continually seen as another; or to the experience of a change in attitude towards the same state of affairs from approval to disapproval or *vice versa*. Yet a categorial change is not, or not only, a change in perception or evaluative attitude. It results in modifying a prior categorization, its associated constitutive or individuating principles or its underlying logic, and is therefore also a change of belief—from belief in one set of propositions to belief in another.

We are on firmer ground when we turn our attention from the experience of categorial change to the propositions and philosophical arguments which are involved in it. For this purpose I shall sketch some examples of competing categorial principles so that when it comes to discussing the rôle of various kinds of philosophical arguments in preserving the old or establishing the new, the discussion does not proceed *in vacuo*.

The first example concerns an aspect of categorial change from pre-Darwinist to Darwinist principles as it occurred for example in Darwin's own mind some time after 1834. All the pre-Darwinist, Christian categorial frameworks acknowledge a maximal kind of souls (spirits) such that (i) the attribute C_1 = 'capable of animating an animal body belonging to a constant created species' (usually, capable of animating a human body) is not empty, and that (ii) being a soul logically implies possessing C_1. It is here not important to ascertain in what form Darwin held this Christian belief. But a note in his diary[1] shows that in 1834 he still believed that all animal species are constant and have been created as such, even though he was by then acquainted with the majority of those observations of comparative anatomy, embryology, geology, of the rudimentary organs of animal species and their geographical distribution which were later to undermine this belief. In abandoning it Darwin was aware of its fundamental position in his categorial framework, as can be seen from the following words taken from a letter written on 11th January, 1844, to Sir Joseph Hooker[2]: 'At last gleams of light have come, and I am almost convinced (quite contrary to the opinion I started with) that species are not (it is like confessing a murder) immutable.'

This Darwinist thesis clearly conflicts with the constitutive principles associated with the maximal kind of souls of pre-Darwinist, Christian categorial frameworks. The conflict can be resolved in a number of ways. The most conservative is to preserve the original maximal kind together with its constitutive principle by either rejecting the Darwinist thesis as false or by regarding it as a merely heuristic principle. A more revolutionary measure would be to modify the original concept of a spirit in accordance with the Darwinist thesis, but to modify it as little as possible. An example of such a modification would consist in replacing the definitional (non-existential) part of the original constitutive principle by: Being a spirit logically implies (in L) being capable of animating a variable species at some specified stage of its evolution which is a process in a created world. The most radical measure is to reject any maximal kind of spirits as empty.

The second example concerns an earlier categorial change from what might be called the Aristotelian to the Newtonian concept of a material

---

[1] *Voyage of a Naturalist Round the World* (London, 1839), ch. XII.

[2] *The Autobiography of Charles Darwin and Selected Letters*, ed. by Francis Darwin (New York, 1892), p. 184.

object, i.e. a solid object movable in space. This change came about partly as a result of accepting the principle of *inertia*, which had been considered by medieval and modern thinkers at least since the days of William of Occam and is the first law of Newton's *Principia*. One of the Aristotelian principles which are constitutive of the older concept of a material object expresses the thesis that (i) the attribute $C_2 = $ 'being incapable of moving without the continual presence of a mover' is not empty and that (ii) being a material object logically implies possessing C_2. The corresponding Newtonian principle which, unlike the Aristotelian, incorporates the principle of *inertia* replaces the definitional part of the Aristotelian principle by: Being a material object logically implies being capable of moving without the continual presence of a mover (namely with uniform speed in a straight line).

The modification of the Aristotelian principle which as a matter of fact became current in post-Newtonian thinking is not the only possible outcome of doubts about the old theories, engendered by reflections on the principle of *inertia* and the phenomena within its scope. Another outcome might have been the complete abandonment of the notion of a material object, for example, in favour of a Leibnizian monadology or a Berkeleyan subjective empiricism; or else the acceptance of the principle of *inertia* as a heuristic principle only.

The third example concerns a fairly recent categorial change from a 'causal' to a 'statistical' concept of an event. This change which has not, or not yet, become part of educated Western common sense came about as the result of persistent failures to incorporate certain experimental findings into classical physics or indeed into any physical theory fitting a categorial framework in which the (or a) principle of causality is constitutive of a maximal kind of events. An early and important phase in the development of the new theory was the resolution in 1900 by Planck of the incompatibility between two equations determining the frequency-distribution of so-called black-body radiation—one of them being approximately confirmed for short wavelengths and low temperatures, the other for long wavelengths and high temperatures. Planck's own equation implied that the radiation has to be accounted for by assuming that energy is absorbed or emitted in discrete quanta and not continuously.

The interpretation of Planck's equation and later equations which around 1925 became part of a unified system of quantum-theory led to the assumption that not only radiation but all phenomena of atomic physics are ultimately statistical, i.e. are subject to probabilistic laws which—unlike the laws of classical statistical mechanics—are incompatible with the assumption of underlying causal laws. Max Born who has had as immediate an experience of this categorial change as Darwin had of an earlier one, recalls it in no less illuminating or vivid a manner.

When the fundamental formula of quantum theory ($p.q - q.p = h/2\pi i$) 'stood before' him he felt, not like a murderer of a venerable old theory, but like 'a mariner who after a long voyage sees the desired land from afar'.[1]

In accepting the principle of ultimately statistical laws of nature Born and his collaborators abandoned a categorial framework which acknowledges a maximal kind of events, one of whose constitutive principles is the following: (i) The attribute C_3 = 'being caused by one or more temporally antecedent events' is not empty; (ii) being an event logically implies (in L) possessing C_3. (The precise nature of the causal determination, e.g. the requirement that it should be representable by second order differential equations, may be left open here.) At the same time they accepted a new constitutive principle in which the definitional part of the principle of causality is replaced by: Being an event logically implies (in L) being probabilistically determined by antecedent events, where the probabilistic determination is to be understood as ultimate and irreducible. It is worth pointing out that in the case of this new and unfamiliar constitutive principle the cautious procedure of its merely heuristic acceptance, which is always possible, has in fact been adopted by some physicists including Planck, Einstein, and Schrödinger who—with Born, Heisenberg, and Jordan—are among the originators of the new theories.

There would be little point in adding further examples of competition between established and new constitutive principles. It is, however, desirable to illustrate briefly how conflicts between a categorial framework and the material which is to be accommodated in it may affect not only the framework's constitutive principles but also its individuating principles or its underlying logic. As regards the modification of individuating principles both the special and the general theories of relativity are suitable examples. Very roughly speaking, the special theory replaces the individuation of events and things in absolute three-dimensional Euclidean space and independent, absolute one-dimensional time by their individuation in a quasi-Euclidean four-dimensional continuum; while the general theory replaces this continuum by a Riemannian four-dimensional continuum with variable curvature (the magnitude of which in a region is identified with the magnitude of a universal force in it).

As regards possible conflicts between the logic underlying a categorial framework and new material, Darwin's theory of evolution and quantum-mechanics may once again serve as illustrations, if we assume that they are considered by a thinker whose primary logic is L. Darwin's thesis of the variability of species implies the impossibility of an exact

[1] Max Born, 'Statistical Interpretation of Quantum Mechanics', *Science*, vol. 122 (1955), pp. 675–679.

distinction between species and varieties because, among other things, 'the amount of difference considered necessary to give any two forms the rank of species cannot be defined'.[1] The need to acknowledge common borderline cases between species and varieties might lead one to replace one's primary logic L by L^*. Some recognition of a conflict between L and Darwin's theory might well lie behind a contemporary biologist's remark that 'if someone should succeed in inventing a universally applicable, static definition of species, he would cast serious doubts on the theory of evolution'.[2] Whether or not the 'proper' interpretation of quantum-mechanics requires or makes desirable the replacement of L by a three-valued logic, as was suggested by von Neumann and Birkhoff, Reichenbach, and others is much less clear.[3]

When a categorial framework comes into conflict with new experience or theories an at least partly adequate alternative may already be available. In Darwin's case this was the theory of Lamarck. But no feasible alternative may be in sight. For such situations it is, in Descartes' words, 'not enough, before commencing to rebuild the house in which we live, that it be pulled down . . . but it is likewise necessary that we be provided with some other house in which we may live conveniently (commodement) during the operations . . .'.[4] During the periods spent in an interim shelter when their old categorial home is no longer inhabitable and a new one is not yet built, people tend to be particularly receptive to philosophical arguments. Yet even in times when a change of categorial framework is not being considered philosophical argument and controversy about it tend to continue.

On the relevance of philosophical arguments to categorial change

Among the characteristically philosophical arguments some are used mainly in support of the categorial *status quo*, others mainly in the cause of categorial revolution, while still others are used opportunistically for either purpose. Since their employment has at times succeeded and at times failed in achieving its end—i.e. preservation, change, or complete abandonment of a hitherto accepted categorial framework—it is at best a contributory factor to it. Yet whether successful or not, all these arguments tend, as a by-product which is incidental to their avowed aim, to clarify the structure of the categorial frameworks whose choice, change, or preservation is at issue, or to present new thought-possibilities previously not available or not recognized.

[1] *The Origin of Species*, 6th edition (London, 1884), p. 47.
[2] T. Dobzhansky, *Evolution, Genetics, Man* (New York, 1955; 7th edition 1966), p. 183.
[3] See, e.g., H. Reichenbach *Philosophic Foundations of Quantum Mechanics* (Berkeley, 1944), §§30 ff.
[4] *Discours de la Méthode*, pt. III.

A type or method of philosophical argument usually advanced in a conservative spirit consists in the explicit articulation of implicit assumptions made by a person and expressed in his speech. Exhibition-analysis, as we may conveniently call it,[1] is as old as the Socratic method, as respectable as Kant's method of metaphysical exposition and as contemporary as the method employed by the late Professor J. L. Austin. And it is no different from these methods. Plato used it when, for example, in the first book of the *Republic* he asks whether Simonides is speaking correctly (ὀρθῶς λέγειν) in saying that 'it is just to render to each his due'. Kant uses it when, for example, in the doctrine of methods of the *Critique of Practical Reason* (Ak. ed. p. 155) he argues that the concept of 'pure morality' is already determined by 'ordinary human reason', not through 'abstract general formulae' but through 'ordinary use, as is the difference between one's right and one's left hand' and that this could be illustrated by an example submitted to 'a ten year old boy for his judgment'. Austin and many others use it when they try to answer philosophical questions by proceeding 'from "ordinary language" that is by examining *what we should say when,* and so why and what we should mean by it'.[2]

The procedure, as applied by the so-called 'ordinary-language' philosophers can be roughly described as follows: If concerned with a philosophical problem or cluster of problems, consider a wide a variety of 'relevant' statements as possible. If any such statement 'in its context' appears 'odd' ('bizarre', 'a category-mistake', etc.) then what it expresses is false or 'unsound'. If any such statement does not appear odd, but its negation does, then what it expresses is true or 'sound'. A native speaker of his language is—after 'suitable training'—capable of judging the relevance, oddity, and soundness in question. The key-terms of this sketch must, because of its brevity, be rather vague and ambiguous. If we assume, as I shall, that the notions can be freed from these shortcomings, their application is nevertheless more limited in scope than its practitioners seem to hold. Ordinary language analysis, like Kant's metaphysical exposition, the Socratic method and any other form of exhibition-analysis merely makes implicit assumptions explicit. It does not render them indispensable, unchangeable, or incorrigible.

It will be sufficient to illustrate this thesis by considering the following statements on the one hand from the point of view of Aristotelian common sense and on the other hand from the point of view of a common sense which has absorbed the assumptions of Darwin's theory of evolution, the general theory of relativity and modern quantum-mechanics. (i) A material object is moving without being moved. (ii) The spatio-temporal interval between two events is for different

---

[1] See, e.g., *What is Philosophy?* (London, 1969), ch. II.
[2] 'A Plea for Excuses' in *Philosophical Papers* (Oxford, 1961), p. 129.

observers given by different lengths and times. (iii) The emission of a particle of radiation is uncaused. (iv) Some of my ancestors are fish. To anybody employing one of the categorial frameworks which were common in ancient and medieval times each of these statements must appear odd, if not downright self-contradictory; whereas to anybody who has accepted the more recent theories of physics and biology as true, rather than as merely heuristically useful, the statements will appear obvious and their negations odd. This impression stems from their function as constitutive principles in these frameworks and their consequent internal incorrigibility with respect to them. The strength of the impression will probably vary according to the degree of firmness with which these principles have taken root in, or have become part of, common sense. An empirical inquiry among contemporary Englishmen would, I should guess, show that many of them would regard (iv) and few of them (ii) as obvious.

Most ordinary-language philosophers seem to regard the exhibition-analysis of 'ordinary language' as philosophically more relevant than the exhibition-analysis of theoretical or technical language. Others seem to ascribe more philosophical relevance to some regions of theoretical or technical language, e.g. the language of law or psychology, than to others.[1] Kant's exhibition-analysis paid particular attention to physics, Aristotle's to educated common sense. These incidental accretions to the method of exhibition-analysis must be distinguished from the method itself which in the hands of philosophers of all ages has served to bring to light implicit assumptions, in particular categorizations and their associated individuating and constitutive principles. By emphasizing the obviousness of the accepted and the oddity of the unaccepted, it tends on the whole towards the preservation of the categorial *status quo*.

Yet exhibition-analysis can be disruptive if it shows, or makes it appear, that the assumptions which it makes explicit are self-contradictory. If such an analysis exhibits a genuine or apparent contradiction which affects a categorial framework, rather than its content, so that abandonment of the framework seems the only way out, it may in accordance with tradition be called an 'aporetic argument'. The most famous aporetic arguments are Zeno's alleged proofs that the concepts of time, change, and motion are self-contradictory and that consequently the perceptions of time, change, and motion are illusory. If one accepts Zeno's arguments, one must abandon the individuating principles associated with any of the notions of physical object so far used (from 'the Stone Age' to Einstein and Bohr), since all of them presuppose that some attribute of spatio-temporal location is not empty and thus *a fortiori* not self-contradictory. If an aporetic argument is fallacious, its contribution to increased clarity can at best be indirect

---

[1] See Austin, op. cit., pp. 123 ff.

6

by giving rise to counter-arguments. Yet in so far as it is convincing it may act as a powerful stimulus for categorial innovation. Whereas Zeno's aporetic arguments are primarily directed against individuating attributes and principles, others are directed against constitutive attributes and principles. Among them are an alleged proof by Leibniz that the notion of material atoms (and of objects made up from them), an alleged proof by Berkeley that the notion of matter and an alleged proof by Bradley that all relations are self-contradictory.

The conservative tendencies of those exhibition-analyses which are not aporetic are sometimes strengthened by what after their most famous instance might be called 'transcendental arguments'. The person propounding a transcendental argument assumes that every and any thinker employs the same categorial framework as he does himself, and tries to show that, and why, the employment of this particular framework is 'necessary'. The defect of all transcendental arguments is their failure to provide a uniqueness-proof, i.e. the demonstration that the categorial framework is universal. Kant and others seem to have been under the illusion that the exhibition of their own categorial framework already includes the proof of its uniqueness.[1]

It would be a mistake to regard all transcendental deductions as wholly obscurantist or barren, even though they are doomed to failure. Kant's transcendental deduction in particular not only sharpens some of the points made in his metaphysical exposition of his categorial framework, but provides together with its preliminaries many of the notions needed for a logico-philosophical inquiry into the structure of categorial frameworks. As remarked earlier, some of these notions, such as those of a category, a constitutive principle, of propositions which are neither empirical nor logical (Kant's synthetic *a priori* propositions), have in a relativized form been used in this essay.

A great deal of philosophical argument is devoted to reconstruction or what by contrast to exhibition-analysis might be called 'replacement-analysis'. It consists, roughly speaking, in replacing defective concepts and assumptions used for certain purposes by sound concepts and assumptions which can be used for the same purposes. Such reconstructive arguments will solve a conflict between a categorial framework and, say, a new theory in favour of one or the other, depending on whatever criteria of soundness are accepted prior to the solution of the conflict. The latitudinarian who, for example, reconstructs his categorial framework rather than Darwin's theory of evolution proceeds in no less logical a manner than the fundamentalist who reconstructs the theory instead. Theory-reconstruction for the sake of the categorial *status quo*

---

[1] See 'The Impossibility of Transcendental Deductions', *Monist*, vol. 51, No. 3, 1967, also 'Transcendental Tendencies in Recent Philosophy' in *Journal of Philosophy*, vol. LXIII, No. 19, 1966.

is always possible since, as we have seen, if all else fails a theory may be demoted from being held as true to being considered as merely of heuristic use.

There are other characteristically philosophical methods. Thus the so-called phenomenological method allegedly describes the common, uninterpreted experience of every and any person; and the so-called dialectical method allegedly anticipates all categorial development. Without going into detailed explanations of these methods,[1] it may be sufficient to point out that the phenomenological method suffers from similar limitations as exhibition-analysis; and that the successful use of the dialectical method requires a uniqueness demonstration the need for which is, as in the case of transcendental argument, ignored by the dialecticians.

It would be out of the question to attempt a complete enumeration of all kinds of philosophical argument and to show for each of them that it does not enable one to prove the truth of one categorial framework over all others. But it is not difficult to see why no argument could ever achieve this. To employ a categorial framework F is to make the following explicit or implicit claims: (i) the plurality of all objects is consistently categorized into non-empty maximal kinds; (ii) with each maximal kind there are associated individuating and constitutive principles, each of which is a conjunction of an existential proposition and a logical implication; (iii) the logical notions used in the formulation of the preceding claims—consistency, logical implication, etc.—are determined by a specific logical theory. To these claims, which can be satisfied by more than one categorial framework, there is sometimes added the uniqueness claim (iv) that only F satisfies the claims (i)–(iii) 'adequately'. Yet unless the adequacy of F is, in circular fashion, defined in terms of F, it could only be established by checking a potentially infinite set of categorial frameworks, some of which are not even known. Any argument attempting this is doomed to failure. But even so it may incidentally clarify old or produce new ideas.

To deny logical cogency to philosophical arguments in support of categorial stability or revolution is thus not to deny them all value or function in categorial change. But if the value of exhibition-analysis, aporetic arguments, transcendental deductions, replacement-analysis, and the rest lies in clarification and the creation of novelty, then it would be mistaken to denigrate unfettered philosophical speculation which, without claiming to prove what is not provable, aims at providing new thought-possibilities. Such avowed, rather than merely incidental, speculation has been the main activity of metaphysicians from the days of the Ionians to the times of McTaggart and Whitehead.

---

[1] See *What is Philosophy?*, ch. II and ch. XIII.

True, some of their proposals for categorial change had to wait a very long time for incorporation into some widely accepted categorial framework, others were at the very best only remote anticipations, while still others—perhaps the majority—are still on the waiting list and might forever stay on it. Again, even if the constitutive and individuating principles of any categorial framework express metaphysical beliefs, and even if in the past metaphysicians have by their theories contributed to the creation of new categorial frameworks, it does not follow that they will continue to do so. But since the opposite does not follow either, a plea for toleration and even encouragement of metaphysical thought-experiments by metaphysicians seems to be a fitting conclusion of this essay.

Appendix

This appendix contains a brief description of the elementary parts, (i.e. propositional logic and quantification-theory) of classical logic (*L*), intuitionist logic (*I*), Ackermann's logic of rigorous implication (*A*), and of certain simple extensions of these systems to neutral propositions and inexact predicates (*L**, *I**, *A**). More complete treatments and bibliographies are found in the works mentioned in the footnotes.

1. The well-formed expressions of L, I, and A

The well-formed formulae of *L*, *I*, and *A* are the same—the differences lying in the valid expressions and formal theorems of these systems. All the following and only the following expressions are well-formed expressions in *L*, *I*, and *A*: (i) Propositional variables, e.g. p, q, r, etc. (ii) n-placed predicate-variables followed by n individual variables, e.g. $P(x)$, $Q(x, y)$, $R(x, y, z)$, etc. Expressions of type (i) and (ii) are called *prime-formulae*; the variables occurring in them are called free (for substitution by constants or binding by quantifiers). (iii) If f is a well-formed expression, then so is $\neg f$. (iv) If f and g are well-formed expressions, then so are $f \wedge g, f \vee g, f \rightarrow g$. (v) If f is a well-formed expression in which x occurs as a free individual variable, briefly if $f(x)$, then so are $\forall x f(x)$ and $\exists x f(x)$. '$\forall x$' is a universal and '$\exists x$' an existential quantifier binding the free variable x of f. Any expression formed by a finite number of applications of (i)–(v) is a well-formed expression. (To be quite precise a bracketing convention would have to be formulated and employed.)

2. The valid expressions, theorems, and logical implications of L

The propositional logic of *L*, i.e. the interpretation of expressions formed in accordance with the rules (i), (iii), and (iv) above, is truth-functional. More precisely the propositional variables range over the values T and F (*true* and *false*); and the value of any compound proposition, which is again T or F, is a function of the truth-values of the components. Thus if p and q are propositional variables $\neg p$ (not-p) is false if p is true and true if p is false; $p \wedge q$ (p and q) is true if p and q are both true, otherwise false; $p \vee q$ (p or q) is false if p and q are both false, otherwise true; $p \rightarrow q$ is false if p is true and q is false, otherwise true; etc. Calling an expression formed in accordance with (i), (iii), and (iv) a (non-quantificational) form, we define such a form as valid if, and only if, every substitution-instance of it is true. (A substitution-instance is the result of substituting true or false propositions for the propositional variables of a form, provided the same substitution is made at every place where the same variable occurs.) A (non-quantificational) proposition is valid if, and only if, it is a substitution-instance of a valid form.

Turning now to well-formed quantificational expressions of L we must distinguish between the 'finite case' in which the individual variables range over a finite domain of individuals and the 'infinite case' in which their range is infinite. In the finite case all universally quantified expressions are interpreted as conjunctions, all existentially quantified expressions as disjunctions. For example, $\forall x P(x)$ becomes $P(x_1) \wedge P(x_2) \wedge \cdots \wedge P(x_n)$, $\exists x P(x)$ becomes $P(x_1) \vee P(x_2) \vee \cdots \vee P(x_n)$ and more complex expressions become more complex truth-functions. In the infinite case we may interpret universally and existentially quantified propositions as 'infinite' conjunctions and disjunctions and introduce other 'infinite' truth-functions. Calling an expression formed in accordance with (i)–(v) a (quantificational) form, we define such a form as valid if, and only if, every substitution-instance of it is true—the substitutions being of propositional, individual, and predicate variables by propositional, individual, and predicate constants. A (quantificational) proposition is valid if, and only if, it is a substitution-instance of a valid form. Our apparent recklessness in speaking of 'infinite' truth-functions can be justified if we can capture all the valid forms in a demonstrably consistent axiomatic theory of L. The following is such a theory.

The axioms are:

(1) $p \rightarrow (p \wedge p)$;   (2) $(p \wedge q) \rightarrow (q \wedge p)$;

(3) $(p \rightarrow q) \rightarrow ((p \wedge r) \rightarrow (q \wedge r))$;

(4) $((p \rightarrow q) \wedge (q \rightarrow r)) \rightarrow (p \rightarrow r)$;

(5) $p \rightarrow (q \rightarrow p)$;   (6) $(p \wedge (p \rightarrow q)) \rightarrow q$;

(7) $p \rightarrow (p \vee q)$;   (8) $(p \vee q) \rightarrow (q \vee p)$;

(9) $((p \rightarrow r) \wedge (q \rightarrow r)) \rightarrow ((p \vee q) \rightarrow r)$;

(10) $\neg p \rightarrow (p \rightarrow q)$;

(11) $((p \rightarrow q) \wedge (p \rightarrow \neg q)) \rightarrow \neg p$;   (12) $p \vee \neg p$;

(13) $\forall x P(x) \rightarrow P(y)$;   (14) $P(y) \rightarrow \exists x P(x)$.

The rules of inference, which we here state without certain more or less obvious provisos, are: (α) the rule of renaming the bound variables of a formula (leading, e.g., from $\exists x P(x) \rightarrow \exists x P(x)$ to $\exists x P(x) \rightarrow \exists y P(y)$); ($\beta$) the rules of substitution for free variables (leading, e.g., from

$\exists zR(x, y, z) \lor \neg\exists zR(x, y, z)$ to $\exists zR(x, x, z) \lor \neg\exists zR(x, x, z))$; ($\gamma$) the rule of substitution for predicate variables (easier to use than to state and leading, e.g., from $\exists x\forall y(P(x,x) \lor \neg P(y,y))$ to $\exists x\forall y(\exists z Q(x,x,z) \lor \exists z Q(y, y, z)))$; ($\delta$) the rule of detachment licensing the inference from the premisses f and $f \to g$ to the conclusion g; (ϵ) the rule licensing the inference from $f \to g(x)$ to $f \to \forall x g(x)$; and (ξ) the rule licensing the inference from $g(x) \to f$ to $\exists x g(x) \to f$.[1]

If we write '$\vdash_L$' in front of any formula which is a theorem in L then the correct transcription of 'Being a P logically implies in L being a Q' is $\vdash_L \forall x(P(x) \to Q(x))$. A correct transcription of 'The attribute C is a constitutive attribute of the maximal kind M in a categorial framework with L as its underlying logic' is $\vdash_L \forall x(M(x) \to C(x))$ where the extensions of M and C are (in accordance with the definition of a maximal kind) neither the empty nor the universal class. The logical implication is consequently neither paradoxical nor trivial. A correct transcription of 'S is a specific individuating subattribute of the general individuating attribute D for M' is $\vdash_L (\forall x(S(x) \to D(x))) \land \forall x\forall y((M(x) \land S(x) \land M(y) \land S(y)) \to (x=y))$, where the extensions of S, D, and M are again neither the universal nor the empty class. The two logical implications are thus again neither trivial nor paradoxical.

3. *The valid expressions, theorems, and logical implications of I*

To accept I is to reject as false or meaningless the assumption of actually infinite sets of objects; consequently of $\forall x P(x)$ and of $\exists x \neg P(x)$ as forms of possibly infinite conjunctions and of possibly infinite disjunctions; consequently of $\forall x P(x) \lor \exists x \neg P(x)$ as a valid form; and thus of axiom (12) in the formal system of L outlined above. Validity in I means constructibility. A valid proposition of I represents the fact that a certain mental construction has been successfully effected in mathematical intuition or some other medium. (See, e.g., Heyting op. cit., p. 8 and pp. 97 ff.) Just as the vague reference to actual infinities which enters the definition of L-validity can be made precise by the formulation of the consistent and complete system L, so the vague reference to constructibilities which enters the definition of I-validity can be made precise by the formulation of a consistent and complete system I. In one of its formulations the system I differs from the system L, as formulated in the preceding section, simply by the omission of axiom (12), i.e. $p \lor \neg p$, from the system of the preceding section.

---

[1] The axioms (1)–(12) are the axioms of Heyting's formalization of intuitionist propositional logic to which (12) the law of excluded middle has been added. The axioms (13) and (14) and the rules (α)–(ξ) are taken from Bernays' formalization of quantification theory. See A. Heyting, *Intuitionism—An Introduction* (Amsterdam, 1956), p. 101, and D. Hilbert and W. Ackermann, *Grundzüge der Theoretischen Logik* (4th edition, Berlin, 1959), p. 90.

If we write '$\vdash_I$' in front of any formula which is a theorem of I, then the correct transcription of 'Being a P logically implies in I being a Q' is $\vdash_I \forall x(P(x) \to Q(x))$. The correct transcriptions of 'The attribute C is a constitutive attribute of the maximal kind M in a categorial framework with I as its underlying logic' and of 'S is a specific individuating sub-attribute of the general individuating attribute D for M' are derived from the corresponding L-transcriptions of the preceding section by simply substituting '$\vdash_I$' for '$\vdash_L$'. It may be worth emphasizing that if the domain of individual objects is assumed to be finite, L and I coincide.

4. The valid expressions, theorems, and logical implications of A

The logical implications by which we defined the notions of constitutive and individuating attributes in L and I express the inclusion of the meaning of their antecedents in the meanings of their consequents only because the extension of M, C, S, D have been assumed to be neither the empty nor the universal class. In general, the logical implications of L and I may be valid without expressing such inclusions of meaning as is seen, for example, in the case $\vdash p \to (q \to p)$ and $\vdash (p \wedge \neg p) \to q$. It is possible to conceive logical implication as a meaning relation ('entail-ment') and to construct formal systems which are in accordance with this requirement. One such system is the system A.[1]

Assuming f, g, h, etc. to be well-formed formulae in accordance with section 1 we present, following Ackermann, the system A in terms of 'axiom-schemata' rather than axioms. The axiom-schemata are:

(1) $f \to f$;
(2) $(f \to g) \to ((g \to h) \to (f \to h))$;
(3) $(f \to g) \to ((h \to f) \to (h \to g))$;
(4) $(f \to (f \to g)) \to (f \to g)$;   (5) $(f \wedge g) \to f$;
(6) $(f \wedge g) \to g$;
(7) $((f \to g) \wedge (f \to h)) \to (f \to (g \wedge h))$;
(8) $f \to (f \vee g)$;   (9) $g \to (f \vee g)$;
(10) $((f \to h) \wedge (g \to h)) \to ((f \vee g) \to h)$;
(11) $(f \wedge (g \vee h)) \to (g \vee (f \wedge h))$;   (12) $(f \to g) \to (\neg g \to \neg f)$;
(13) $(f \wedge \neg g) \to \neg(f \to g)$;   (14) $f \to \neg \neg f$;
(15) $\neg \neg f \to f$;   (16) $(f \to \mathbb{A}) \to \neg f$;
(17) $(f \wedge \neg f) \to \mathbb{A}$;

(The sign '$\mathbb{A}$' is a constant interpreted as 'the absurd'; so that if '$f \to \mathbb{A}$', i.e. f implies the absurd, is interpreted as f is impossible.)

(18) $\forall x f(x) \to f(y)$;   (19) $f(y) \to \exists x f(x)$;
(20) $\forall x(g \to f(x)) \to (g \to \forall x f(x))$;
(21) $\forall x(f(x) \to g) \to (\exists x f(x) \to g)$;

[1] See W. Ackermann, 'Begründung einer strengen Implikation', *Journal of Symbolic Logic*, vol. 21, No. 2 (1956).

(22) $\forall x(f(x) \vee g) \rightarrow \forall x f(x) \vee g$;
(23) $(g \wedge \exists x f(x)) \rightarrow \exists x(g \wedge f(x))$.

The rules of inference, which we state without certain more or less obvious provisos, are: (α) the rule of detachment licensing the inference from the premisses f and $f \rightarrow g$ to the conclusion g; (β) the rule licensing the inference from the premisses f and g to the conclusion $(f \wedge g)$; (γ) the rule licensing the inference from the premisses $f \rightarrow g$ and $((f \rightarrow g) \wedge h) \rightarrow \mathbb{A}$ to $h \rightarrow \mathbb{A}$; (δ) the rule of licensing the inference from the premiss $f(x)$ to the conclusion $\forall x f(x)$; (ϵ) the rule for renaming bound and free variables.

If we write '$\vdash_A$' to indicate that a formula preceded by it is a theorem we arrive at the correct transcriptions in A of the expressions, which at the end of sections (2) and (3) were transcribed into L and I, by simply substituting A for L (or I). Ackermann's system is an attempt at capturing an intuitive sense of (non-trivial and non-paradoxical) 'entailment' which in some ways is more successful than C. I. Lewis' systems of strict implication.[1]

5. The valid expressions, theorems, and logical implications of L^*, I^*, A^*

We extend L to L^* by allowing for inexact predicates, i.e. predicates which apart from (clearly) positive and negative cases also have neutral or borderline cases, i.e. cases to which the predicate can with equal correctness be assigned or refused. With regard to neutral cases of a predicate we may thus distinguish two stages, namely a *provisional* stage in which an object is recognized as neutral and a *final* stage in which a decision is taken to turn it into a positive or a negative case. Using letters with subscripts for constants and letters without subscripts for variables, we indicate that an object x_0 is a neutral case for a predicate P_0 be writing: $*P_0(x_0)$; and we similarly indicate the neutrality of an atomic proposition p_0 by writing: $*p_0$. In the provisional stage a proposition may have the truth-values T (true), F (false), and U (neutral)—the last being turned in the final stage into either T or F. The truth-tables for the provisional stage are given by Kleene. They are as follows:

Table for $\neg p$		*Table for* $p \wedge q$				*Table for* $p \vee q$			
				q				q	
p	$\neg p$		T	F	U		T	F	U
T	F	$\ \ \lceil T$	T	F	U	$\ \ \lceil T$	T	T	T
F	T	$p \lbrace F$	F	F	F	$p \lbrace F$	T	F	U
U	U	$\ \ \lfloor U$	U	F	U	$\ \ \lfloor U$	T	U	U

---

[1] See C. I. Lewis and C. H. Langford, *Symbolic Logic* (New York, 1932); R. Feys, *Modal Logics* (Louvain, Paris, 1965).

Table for $p \to q$ | Table for $p \leftrightarrow q$

		q		
		T	F	U
p	T	T	F	U
	F	T	T	T
	U	T	U	U

		q		
		T	F	U
p	T	T	F	U
	F	F	T	U
	U	U	U	U

The tables are extensions of the truth-tables for L in the sense that if we eliminate the third rows and the third columns—the U-rows and the U-columns—we arrive at the truth-tables for L. In conformity with the truth-tables for conjunction and disjunction we define $\forall x P_0(x)$ as true if, and only if, all objects are positive cases of $P_0(x)$; as false if, and only if, at least one object is a negative case of $P_0(x)$; as neutral if, and only if, at least one object is a neutral case and the others are neutral or positive cases of $P_0(x)$. And we define $\exists x P_0(x)$ as true if, and only if, at least one object is a positive case of $P_0(x)$; as false if, and only if, all objects are negative cases of $P_0(x)$; and as neutral if, and only if, at least one object is a neutral case and the others are neutral or negative cases of $P_0(x)$.[1]

L^* contains no valid—i.e. identically true—*forms* (expressions containing at least one free variable). Thus for $p = U$ the truth-value of $\neg(p \land \neg p)$ is by the truth-tables for negation and conjunction itself U. It is nevertheless possible to define the validity of *propositions* of L^* in terms of the logical validity of corresponding propositions of L. One intuitively attractive possibility is to require for the validity of a proposition of L^* that (i) its non-neutral, definite, or exact core be valid in L and (ii) that, however one turns the neutral components of the proposition of L^* into definite propositions, the resulting propositions be valid in L. This can be made more precise, for example in the following way.

Let us write f_0 for a proposition, as opposed to a form, of L^*. Let us similarly write $p_0, q_0, \ldots$ for the (definite or indefinite) atomic propositions, and $P_0(x)$, $Q_0(x, y), \ldots$ for the (exact or inexact) predicates, which occur in f_0 as its prime components. We define (i) 'the definite core of f_0', briefly $[f_0]$, as the result of eliminating from f_0 all neutral *atomic* propositions and all inexact predicates (together with the connectives and quantifiers which thereby become superfluous); (ii) 'a definite evaluation of f_0'—say, $Ev_1(f_0)$, $Ev_2(f_0), \ldots$—as any proposition derived from f_0 by assigning to every indefinite atomic proposition of f_0 a definite truth-value (i.e. truth or falsehood) and by regarding every neutral case of an inexact predicate of f_0 as a definite (i.e. positive or negative) case of it. For example, if $f_0 = p_0 \lor \neg p_0 \lor q_0$ with $p_0 = U$

[1] See S. C. Kleene, *Introduction to Metamathematics* (Amsterdam, 1952), esp. §64, and S. Körner, *Experience and Theory*, ch. III.

and $q_0 = T$, then $[f_0] = q_0$, $Ev_1(f_0) = p_0 \lor \neg p_0 \lor q_0$ with $p_0 = T$ and $q_0 = T$, $Ev_2(f_0) = p_0 \lor \neg p_0 \lor q_0$ with $p_0 = F$ and $q_0 = T$. Every proposition has at most one definite core and at most a finite number of definite evaluations.

Before defining the validity of a proposition f_0 in L^* in terms of the validity of its definite core and its definite evaluations in L, we observe that any particular definite evaluation of f_0 is valid in L if, and only if, every definite evaluation of f_0 is valid in L. (This follows from the definition of a proposition as valid in L if, and only if, it is a substitution-instance of a valid form of L.) We may thus choose any one of the definite evaluations of f_0 as representing all of them—for example, the evaluation which results from assigning the value *truth* to every indefinite atomic proposition of f_0 and from regarding every neutral case of an inexact predicate of f_0 as a positive case of it. Let us call this definite evaluation of f_0 'the representative definite evaluation' or, briefly 'the definite evaluation' of f_0 and write $[\![f_0]\!]$ for it.

We can now, in terms of its definite core and its definite evaluation, define the validity of f_0 in L^* as follows: $\vdash_{L^*} f_0$ if, and only if, $\vdash_L [f_0]$ and $\vdash_L [\![f_0]\!]$. In words, a proposition is valid in L^* if, and only if, its definite core and its definite evaluation are valid in L, i.e. if, and only if, each of them is a substitution-instance of a valid form of L. (The proposition of our example is thus not valid in L^* because its definite core is not valid in L.) The definition of logical implication in L^* takes the form $\vdash_{L^*} (f_0 \to g_0)$. What has been said about the definition of constitutive and individuating attributes in a categorial framework with underlying logic L^* holds *mutatis mutandis* in a categorial framework with underlying logic L^*.

Just as L can be extended to L^* by allowing for inexact predicates and neutral propositions, so I can be extended to I^* and A to A^*. As regards a suitable definition of the validity of propositions in I^* and A^* one will again have to consider the non-neutral core, if any, of propositions and the way in which they are affected by the definite evaluation of their neutral prime components. We shall have $\vdash_{I^*} f_0$ if, and only if, $\vdash_I [f_0]$ and $\vdash_I [\![f_0]\!]$; and $\vdash_{A^*} f_0$ if, and only if, $\vdash_A [f_0]$ and $\vdash_A [\![f_0]\!]$. Similar considerations apply to the modal logics of C. L. Lewis and to other logical systems.[1]

---

[1] Compare J. P. Cleave, 'The Notion of Validity in Logical Systems with Inexact Predicates' forthcoming in *British Journal for the Philosophy of Science*.

UNIVERSITY OF BRISTOL

Department of Philosophy

9 Woodland Road
Bristol
BS8 1TB

Index

83